Spontaneous
Performance
Acting through Improv

Marsh Cassady

MERIWETHER PUBLISHING LTD.
Colorado Springs, Colorado

Meriwether Publishing Ltd., Publisher
P.O. Box 7710
Colorado Springs, CO 80933

Editor: Theodore O. Zapel
Typesetting: Elisabeth Hendricks
Cover design: Janice Melvin

Library of Congress Cataloging-in-Publication Data

Cassady, Marsh, 1936-
    Spontaneous performance : acting through improv / by Marsh Cassady.–1st ed.
    p.cm.
    Includes bibliographical references.
    ISBN 1-56608-064-9 (pbk.)
        1. Improvisation (Acting) [1. Plays--Improvisation. 2. Acting--Technique.] I. Title.

PN2071.I5 C28 2000
792'.028--dc21

                        00-041894

1 2 3 4 5 6 7 8   00 01 02 03

Acknowledgments

Thanks to Jim Kitchen for his help with the editing of the book and to John Stevanus for his help with getting the books I needed to complete it. Thanks to José Navarro for allowing me to photograph and use reproductions of the paintings in the book, and to the models who posed for the photos: Kathryn Cogswell (and Gato), Taylor Johnson, Jim Kitchen, Arlene Siemen, Ellen Snortland, and John Stevanus.

*To John Stevanus
and in memory of Nate Bishop*

Contents

Preface

For the Teacher

There can be several definitions of improvisation. For the purposes of this book, I'm defining it as spontaneous acting which can — but does not always have to — result in a presentation before an audience.

Spontaneous Performance is intended as a companion book or sequel to *Acting Games, Improvisations and Exercises.* Although it is desirable that those working with the book be acquainted with the sorts of acting games and exercises I included in the first book so that they have a background in spontaneity, this is not absolutely necessary. That is, *Spontaneous Performance* can easily stand on its own. However, I feel that if students don't have such experience, they should learn a little bit about the basics of physically and mentally preparing themselves for doing improvisations, and further, that they make a habit of practicing such exercises. To this end, perhaps the teacher can review materials relating to these two concepts in *Acting Games* or other similar books so that each class session can begin with five minutes of warm-up exercises.

Included in the book are exercises intended to lead to many different types of improvisation, from scenes dealing with the problems of young people to improvising with existing drama or play texts to improvising and polishing original plays.

The improvisations are all easily producible, requiring only simple sets and props.

Improvisation should be fun. It also is an extremely valuable way to develop confidence, to build characters, and to understand the various aspects of acting and drama.

Of necessity, there are some techniques and exercises that the teacher or student familiar with *Acting Games* will recognize. This occurs only occasionally, and in nearly every case these concepts are taken much further toward actual performance than were the exercises in *Acting Games.*

Also, since this book builds upon certain concepts from *Acting Games,* I have included a few brief explanations similar to a few of those in the earlier book. These can serve to refresh the memories of those familiar with *Acting Games* and to acquaint those who have not used the previous book with facts and concepts they need to understand to proceed with the exercises in *Spontaneous Performance.*

Introduction

To the Actor

The purpose of this book is to help you develop your creative abilities and talents in presenting improvisations. Thus there are a wide variety of exercises that range from the serious to the ridiculous.

The book is divided into four sections, each dealing with a different type of improvisation. As you go through each section, you will receive tips on how to present the scene. But just as important as anything else, remember that the exercises should be fun.

Part One contains suggestions for various types of conflict among individuals. Part Two deals with reactions leading to conflict with obstacles such as existing conditions, beliefs, and the environment. Part Three has exercises involving physical positions, objects, and random lines as the basis of scenes and monologs, while Part Four will show you ways to use improv to better understand existing plays and finally to improvise an original play.

Spontaneous Performance gives more space to activities than to text, particularly after the first few chapters. This is because, in large part, a person learns to be creative and to act by "doing" rather than reading about how to do it.

As you try each activity, remember that first of all you should have fun, which in this class should be your most important goal. The rest will follow naturally.

Reasons for Doing Improv

As you begin this course, you may wonder why you should participate in improvisational theatre. One reason is that these activities involve you immediately without your having to go to auditions, learn lines, and spend hours learning blocking

1

(movement). Besides, they teach the need to watch, listen, and pay attention, rather than just to stare and wait, as actors unfortunately do sometimes in a play. Improv also can sharpen acting skills and expand your ability to play a variety of roles.

The improvs do not require long rehearsals and planning, which means that everyone gets a turn at doing many different kinds. The exercises should give you ideas for developing further improvisations. You do not need to be bound by what is included in the book. Feel free to come up with your own exercises for each of the categories.

Improv can be performed in nearly any type of space — a classroom, a gym, or a stage. You don't even need much in the way of furniture or properties. It is a good idea if you have a few chairs that can be moved around, and a table and desk. Occasionally, you will be asked to bring objects from home. Or if you have access to your school's property room, that will often do just as well or better.

Part One

Improvisational Conflict among Individuals

Chapter One

Improvs for Developing Conflict

Theatre reflects life, which is filled with conflicts, both big and small. This means that much of theatre and drama are made up of placing characters in situations where they clash with other people or things.

Teenagers clash with parents, with teachers, with others in authority, with friends, with peers, and with siblings. That's human nature. Since improvisation often is a play in miniature, it stands to reason that it most often involves a clash between opposing sides.

How often have you felt irritation at a friend who simply will not accept what you say, or believe, or want to do, even though you think it's the most logical thing on earth? The first set of exercises involves this sort of irritation that can be mild or lead to something far greater than it ever started out to be. These scenes, like the others in this chapter, are pretty straightforward and uncomplicated to get you used to getting up in front of an audience. In later chapters, they will involve more characters and more complicated circumstances. Do keep in mind when doing improvisation that disagreement and conflict, although similar, are not the same thing. For instance, the following does not cause a scene to build. It's just an argument:

"You stole my pencil."
"I did not."
"You did too."
"Did not."
"You borrowed it yesterday and didn't give it back."
"I gave it back."
"Did not."

5

And so on. There's little point in this sort of thing unless it quickly leads to something else.

Short but Not So Sweet

The improv scenes involve conflict or a clash of wills over things that are relatively unimportant. As with all improvisations involving conflict, try to bring them to a logical but simple conclusion, which probably will involve compromise — just as in life we often are forced to compromise when things don't go the way we want them to go.

Don't try to make more of the scenes than they are worth; don't drag them out. Each should last no more than a minute or so. They're the sort of situations that in real life probably would soon be forgotten. Though fairly trivial, they involve a variety of subjects and a variety of characters. When names are not given, you are free to come up with your own. Also, when anything else is vague or nonspecific, you can make of it what you like. In Exercise 4, for example, the team can be basketball, volleyball, swimming, or anything else that fits. In fact, you can add whatever you like to a scene so long as it is consistent with the information that is provided.

1. You are best friends and agree on almost anything. Both of you saw last night's TV movie and amazingly one of you loved it, and the other hated it. It's the following morning, and you two meet outside school as you do every day. Each of you can hardly wait to ask the other's opinion of the movie.

2. On the way home from school, one of you buys the other a vanilla ice cream cone. The one who buys the cone knows very well, but may have forgotten, that the other one can't stand vanilla.

3. You and your friend plan to go to a movie. One of you wants to see the newest space opera. The other hates science fiction and wants to see that new horror film. The science fiction buff has seen

one horror movie and has vowed never to see another. You are both in the ticket line at the theatre where the two films are being shown.

4. One of you is trying out for the school team. The other, though good in sports, isn't interested. The first pleads with the second one that the team really needs him or her.

5. The two of you are best friends and do most things together. The town's fall festival is coming up this weekend. There are lots of booths and all sorts of entertainment. One of you wants to go. The other didn't do so well on the last math quiz and thinks the weekend should be devoted to study. The one who wants to attend the festival pleads with the other to go along.

Why is conflict important in drama? If everything ran smoothly, there would be little reason to present a play. Certainly, in real life, things are more pleasant if there are no disagreements, no bickering, and no arguments, and if people don't get angry or upset with each other. But in a play it would be boring.

Imagine even a one-act in which everyone agrees with everyone else, no matter what is suggested. In such a case, there could be no real differences in personality and outlook. Everyone would be pretty much like everyone else. At best, a play that showed this sort of situation would be funny. But before too long, the humor probably would begin to fade.

So what does happen in a scene or a play? The central character is presented with a problem. This occurs early on. The rest of the play, whether a couple of minutes or a couple of hours long, shows how the character deals with the problem, which always involves one side against the other.

Sometimes conflict involves one person against another or others. Sometimes it is a person against a part of self or even against a condition or a force, such as nature. For instance, a character gets no enjoyment out of life because he or she always looks on the negative side of everything. The character is determined to change his or her thinking but finds it is difficult. Or a character against a force of nature could be the story of someone stranded on a cliff in a snowstorm.

The improvisations in this chapter, however, all deals with characters in conflict with each other.

Scenes of conflict always have to come to a satisfactory ending. In a TV mystery series, this often means that the bad guy is caught and sentenced to prison. But in the exercises so far and in most that follow, there are no bad guys. There simply are people who disagree. So for these, there can be no sense of defeat as there often is for the bad guy in a TV show. Rather the scene should come to an ending that is satisfactory to both sides.

For instance, a logical ending to the second of the following problems is that the person who cannot stand any noise or distractions while studying decides either to wear earplugs or to study in the family car out in the driveway. But for a logical ending, the one who needs the music also has to give a little. For instance, he or she might say something like: "If you agree to let me have the music on tonight, I promise I'll do my studying for the next four weeks when you're at work."

Still Short and Sweet but More Involved

The following improvisations shouldn't take more than a minute or two. You can approach them in one of two ways. You can simply begin without any preparation, or if you wish, you can talk for thirty seconds with your partner to plan out a scenario. You may want to experiment with each of these methods.

1. The characters include a girl and a boy. Here is the situation.

GIRL: Your best friend is appearing in her first skating competition. You cannot take time from school to travel to another location to watch in person, but the competition is being televised by the local cable channel. Not only do you want to watch, but you promised your friend that you would. Your brother insists on watching a news magazine.

BOY: In social studies class, students have volunteered to

watch various news magazines such as *Sixty Minutes* and *20/20* and then to report on them in class. The show you've volunteered to watch is on at the same time as the skating competition your sister wants to watch.

The action begins when the boy comes into the room where the girl has just turned on the television set.

Two or three sets of students can do the above exercise for which there can be several good solutions. See how many different ideas you can come up with in bringing the conflict in all the exercises to a satisfactory ending.

2. The characters are either two girls or two boys.

The two of you share a bedroom. One of you needs music in order to concentrate. The other cannot study if there's even the slightest distraction. The rest of the house is noisy because your parents have dinner guests. Finals begin tomorrow, and for whatever reason, neither of you has done much studying. How can each of you be sure you're prepared?

3. The characters include you and another person of your choice. The big spring dance is coming up in just a few months. You really want to go with that special person in your life. But you have very little spending money, and certainly not enough for the dance. You've applied for a job as a bagger at the supermarket but have almost given up on getting it. Yet you know if you don't, there's no way you can go to the dance.

You've also been doing some baby-sitting, but that certainly isn't steady enough to provide the money you need. The couple for whom you've been baby-sitting almost exclusively has planned a big night out to celebrate their wedding anniversary. An hour before you're due at their house, the manager of the supermarket calls and says you have the job. The trouble is you have to start immediately. You have to be down at the store in less than an hour.

Decide whether you want to talk with the store manager about this or whether you want to discuss it with the couple who's expecting you to baby-sit. Take a minute or so to talk with the person(s) you choose.

4. Characters include you and your mother OR you and your date. You need to choose which.

The championship game is coming up this weekend. Not only that, but you have a date to attend with the person you've been wanting to go out with for nearly two years. The thing is, it's your grandmother's birthday, and the family is throwing a surprise party. Everyone is expected to attend. You're torn about what to do; you love your grandmother, but this is THE championship game, and you do have a really important date.

If you've chosen to do the scene with your mother, it now might be interesting to see what happens when you play it with your date. If you've chosen the date first, now you can try the scene with the mother.

5. You've just taken your first final of the semester. Another student whom you like and want to get to know better is certain that he or she saw you cheating on the exam. Try to convince this other person that you were not cheating.

There are many plays that do not have conflict, but rather have other characteristics that hold an audience's interest. In later chapters you will be doing improvisations involving scenes that fit into these sorts of situations.

Humor in Improvs

So far you probably have tried to present serious scenes of conflict. But for the next series of exercises, try to make them as funny as you can.

Take a minute or two with your partner to plan out the direction you want to take with the scenes and try to determine what sorts of things you can do to make them funny.

1. CHARACTER 1: Your cousin, whom you haven't seen in ten years, is flying into town. Since both your mom and dad will be at work when the plane arrives, they've asked you to meet this

cousin, who is of the opposite sex.

CHARACTER 2: You have just flown into town to meet with your cousin whom you haven't seen in six or seven years. Character 1 approaches you and asks if you're the cousin he or she was to pick up. This person, however, is much, much different from the cousin you remember. Actually, this isn't your cousin but another person who has come to pick up somebody else.

The scene begins when Character 1 approaches Character 2 at the airport.

2. CHARACTER 1: You're walking out of school beside the person of the opposite sex whom you really want to impress. The person tells you that your shoelace is untied. You bend down to tie it, and the back seam in your jeans splits. You are really embarrassed and want to conceal from the other person what happened.

CHARACTER 2: You are acquainted with Character 1, but don't know the person well. However, you've hoped for a chance to know him or her better. Now you find that all of a sudden this person is acting very strangely. You don't understand why. Maybe he or she is really weird ... and you should leave. However, you're not sure how to get away without appearing rude.

3. CHARACTER 1: You realize after a few minutes at what you think is a surprise birthday party for your best friend, that you're at the wrong place. This is a surprise party all right, but it's for someone else, someone you've disliked for years and who strongly dislikes you. You try to sneak out but are cornered by the other person's mother who wonders why you are leaving.

CHARACTER 2: You see Character 1 trying to sneak out. You'd seen this character arriving and were pleased because you thought this meant that the two teenagers (your son or daughter) finally had patched up their differences. You want to make certain that Character 1 feels welcome.

4. CHARACTER 1: Another student whom you know slightly congratulates you for winning the award for outstanding student of the year. You did not win the award even though you thought you might. You're even a little resentful that you didn't win.

CHARACTER 2: Just after offering your congratulations to Character 1, you realize you've made a mistake. This is really Pat Smith, and not Pat Jones. You've always had a hard time remembering which name belongs to which person.

5. GIRL: You receive a note asking you to attend the big dance at school. You are thrilled since the boy who wrote the note is someone you definitely want to get to know better.

BOY: You've finally gotten up your nerve to ask a girl to the school dance. You asked a friend to pass on a note to her. Your friend asks another person to deliver the note which gets into the wrong hands. You don't know the note was mis-sent.

The scene begins when the two of you meet in the hall after school.

The Comic Versus the Serious

Depending on your intent and the way you approach a scene, you often can take the same set of circumstances, the same characters, and the same beginning incident and make a scene either funny or serious. Play one or more of the following in a serious way and then in a comic way. Take two or three minutes with your partner to plan each way of presenting a scene.

1. CHARACTER 1: At the dance competition for which there is a $100 prize, you and your partner got you feet tangled and nearly fell down. You really expected to win and are very upset.

CHARACTER 2: Though your partner blames you for what happened on the dance floor, you are certain it isn't your fault.

2. GIRL: You accept a date to the prom because the person you wanted to go with hasn't asked you. Just after you say yes, he does ask. You are happy that he finally asked but angry that it took

so long, and that you now have a dilemma to deal with.

BOY: You weren't sure you would be able to attend the prom. When you find out that you can, you ask the girl whom you like.

The scene begins when the BOY asks the GIRL to go with him.

3. CHARACTER 1: You are taking a friend to the mall in a nearby city to hang out and later go to a movie. For the second time in a row, you've forgotten to buy gas before leaving town. Now the car has died on a lonely stretch of road.

CHARACTER 2: You are exasperated because this is the second time your friend has run out of gas. Besides that, you had really been looking forward to seeing the movie. This is the last day it will be shown.

4. BOY: You are supposed to take your date to the big event at school. But outside your house you have slipped in the wet grass and fallen. Your clothes are covered with mud, and you have nothing else to wear. You think the best thing to do is to go to your date's house and explain what has happened.

GIRL: You have very much been looking forward to the school event. All of your friends will be there. You don't know what to think when your date shows up covered in mud.

This exercise is a little bit difficult in that it depends entirely on how you approach it. If the boy is apologetic and the girl understanding, the scene won't go much of anywhere. However, if, for instance, the boy treats what happened as a joke or as if it's no big deal, and the girl is not at all understanding, there's a better basis for conflict. This means that the character you choose to assume determines to a large extent both the direction of the scene and the emotional pitch.

5. CHARACTER 1: You must explain to a sibling how you mistakenly used his or her history report, due today, to line the bird cage.

CHARACTER 2: You worked for days on your history report and are certain you've done the best you can. You really need to do well on it because lately your history grade has been slipping.

Playing with Dead Seriousness

Analyze what you did to make the scene funny. To make it serious. How successful were you? When performing improv, it often is easier to make a scene come across as funny than to keep it serious.

You often can make an unrealistic scene come across as funnier if you play it in dead seriousness. Try that with the following.

1. CHARACTER 1: You are inconsolable because you broke your fingernail.

CHARACTER 2: You understand the seriousness of the problem and try to find a way to help. It's very difficult to do that.

2. CHARACTER 1: You are trying to put an end to violence in the world by inventing a "nice pill" that everyone will be required to take.

CHARACTER 2: You are worried that your friend is working much too hard at developing this pill and try to convince him or her to take it easy.

3. CHARACTER 1: Although you've never participated in athletics of any kind, you are convinced that all you need to do is practice your running all day long every day in order to make it to the next Olympics.

CHARACTER 2: Although you do agree that perhaps your friend can easily become an Olympic champion, you are worried that the exercising which always leaves him or her on the brink of exhaustion will lead to serious physical problems.

4. CHARACTER 1: You want to bury the latest dead body in the basement of your cousin's house.

CHARACTER 2: You try to convince your cousin that it's always best to bury dead bodies in the back yard. You give him or her all the reasons that you believe this is so.

5. CHARACTER 1: You are an alien from outer space who could hardly wait to get out of your space ship in order to use a

bathroom. The trouble is, even if you find a bathroom, you have never quite understood how those on earth work. You knock on a door. An earth creature (a member of one of the opposite sexes from yours) opens the door.

CHARACTER 2: An alien knocks on the door and asks to use the bathroom. Although you are startled by its appearance, you can see how badly it is in need. You agree to let it in. It thanks you but says you will have to explain how earth bathrooms work.

Exaggerated Traits

Exaggerating a particular trait can make it funny. This can be even funnier when others in the scene react to the trait in dead seriousness.

1. CHARACTER 1: You are a hypochondriac who lists one problem (such as a headache, a sore back, a stomach ache, etc.) after another.

CHARACTER 2: You are sympathetic and try to think of ways of helping your friend with the various problems. However, he or she is sure that none of your suggestions will help. It's up to you to determine how to react to this.

2. CHARACTER 1: You are extremely lazy and haven't done your chores. In fact, all you want to do is slouch around, lie on the sofa, or curl up in the chair. You do these various things as your friend, who is very industrious, talks to you.

CHARACTER 2: You try to explain to your friend in a rational way all the reasons why it is important for him or her to do the assigned chores.

3. CHARACTER 1: You are a glutton who eats everything in sight. This includes your best friend's share of the pizza. As he or she talks to you, you continue to stuff yourself.

CHARACTER 2: You try to convince your best friend that overeating is bad for your health. All the while, you are very hungry.

4. CHARACTER 1: You are easily distracted. In fact, your attention span often is nonexistent. You simply do not or cannot listen to others or pay attention. You are rarely in the here and now. Because of this you are losing friends who are tired of what seems to be your lack of interest in them.

CHARACTER 2: Character 1 is your best friend, and you want to help the person conquer the habit of not paying attention. Well, it's not a matter of not paying attention, it is a matter of paying attention to too many things, switching quickly from one to the other. The kindest thing you can say is that your friend is easily distracted. You want to try to get the person to change since no one tries to be friends with him or her anymore.

As you learned in the introduction, improvisation serves many different purposes. In the next chapter, you will explore these purposes further.

Chapter Two

Comedy Improv through Conflict

One of the reasons for using improv in class is to let you, as an actor, become used to a variety of situations. This is important because it builds confidence and assures you that you will be able to handle a wide range of characters and situations in plays.

Silly but Normal

The following exercises are just plain silly. Remember, however, that a good way to make them come across that way is to play them as if the situation were normal. Each of these should take one to two minutes to present.

1. CHARACTER 1: You just looked into the mirror and are convinced you are turning blue. You don't want to turn blue but don't know how to reverse the process. You need to convince your best friend that what is happening is true so that the friend can help you change back.

CHARACTER 2: You believe what your best friend says about turning blue. You desperately want to help the person find a way to reverse the process and change back to his or her original color, green.

2. CHARACTER 1: You have discovered undeniable proof that your parents are space aliens who adopted you in order to fit in better on earth as an average family. You don't know what their motive is in doing this, and you don't want to bring harm to them. All the same, you realize that you have to expose them for what they are since aliens are trying to take over the world. You need to ask a friend for advice, and then the two of you need to figure out whether or not to notify the government of your discovery.

CHARACTER 2: Your friend tells you that his parents are space aliens. Although you don't doubt your friend's word, you have mixed feelings about the situation. This is because you've always liked the parents. In fact, of all the adults you know outside your family, they are your favorites. You also know there are good aliens who want to prevent earth's takeover, and bad ones. You are certain your friend's parents are the former.

3. CHARACTER 1: You show your friend that you have discovered how to use your own powers to fly. It's simple. Now you want to convince everyone that this is the best way to travel.

CHARACTER 2: Your friend proves to you that he or she has learned how to fly and wants to teach you. You, however, are convinced that you're such a klutz you could never learn. The friend keeps insisting and trying to teach you, but you also are afraid of heights.

4. CHARACTER 1: You have discovered that the neighbor's dog is a foreign spy and that you are responsible for breaking the code the dog barks each night to the enemy. You try to get a friend to help you.

CHARACTER 2: Your friend wants you to help break the barking code of the dog next door since the friend believes the dog is a foreign spy sent to gather information vital to U.S. security. You, on the other hand, know that the dog is a CIA agent and that he is being kept prisoner next door, as witnessed by the long chain attached to his collar. You must decide how best to help this dog, how to convince your friend that he or she is wrong, and finally to get the person to help you. Each of you needs to offer proof that what you believe is true.

5. You know that it isn't only green plants that need to experience photosynthesis. This is because the planet is running out of oxygen, and no one else seems to be doing anything about it. You know that by harvesting leaves from trees, making juice from them, and drinking this juice will help human beings to

undergo photosynthesis and thus give off oxygen, enough, in fact, to save the planet from disaster. It is very important that you convince everyone of this, beginning with Character 2.

CHARACTER 2: You already know that in order to provide enough oxygen for everyone, you need to undergo photosynthesis. You have discovered that the way to do this is to wear only green clothing and to stand out in the sun for an hour or two each day, longer, of course, when it's cloudy. You need to convince Character 1 to help you spread the word about what you've learned.

Each of you needs to convince the other that your way is the correct one.

Strange but Not True

In the foregoing exercises, both characters had strange beliefs and feelings. Those that follow are a little different in that here only one of the characters in each exercise has a strange quirk.

1. CHARACTER 1: You are completely thrilled at being able to have a pet honeybee, the queen at that. You can hardly wait to show your best friend the new pet.

CHARACTER 2: Your friend arrives with a new "pet," a honeybee and is thrilled at being able to keep it. You think this is the most ridiculous thing you've ever heard, and to complicate matters, you are really afraid of bees. But Character 1, after all, is your best friend.

One of the most important outcomes of the improv is that the two characters remain friends.

2. CHARACTER 1: You are absolutely ecstatic because you've been notified that you've been selected as Outstanding Nerd of the Year. This is the first important award you've ever received, and you can hardly contain yourself. You want to share the news with your best friend, who you know will be just as happy about it as you are.

CHARACTER 2: Your friend tells you about being chosen Outstanding Nerd of the Year. You simply cannot believe that anyone would want such an award.

3. CHARACTER 1: You have learned that your best friend finally has a date with a certain person of the opposite sex, a person your friend has liked for years. You are so happy about this that you plan to throw a big party of celebration, inviting all your mutual friends. Your friend and his or her date will be guests of honor.

CHARACTER 2: You've liked a certain person of the opposite sex for years and are thrilled that the two of you now are going on your first date. You've told your best friend about this since he/she has always known how you felt about the person you'll be dating. Now Character 2 plans to throw a party to celebrate that you and the other person finally are getting together. Of course, this party would be the most embarrassing thing you can imagine, and you don't understand why your friend would consider doing such a thing. Actually, the invitations already may have been delivered.

4. CHARACTER 1: You've worked for a long time to collect different colors of dirt. Dust from Arizona, red earth from Georgia, rich loam from Minnesota, and so on. You are proud of the big pile of it that you've now dumped in the middle of your living room. When a friend visits, you want to explain the significance of this big mound of earth.

CHARACTER 2: You go to visit your friend and see a big pile of dirt in the middle of the living room floor. You try to ignore it, but your friend insists you look closely. You think the friend is insane when he or she tries to explain how important the dirt is and then expresses pride at having it there. You want to convince your friend that most people want to get rid of dirt and that collecting it is insane.

5. CHARACTER 1: You want to be a fashion trend-setter and so try to convince everyone, beginning with a close friend, that wearing completely mismatched clothing soon will be all the rage.

CHARACTER 2: When your friend tells you about the new fashion revolution, consisting of wearing totally mismatched clothes, you think the person is nuts, and you try to convince him or her not to go through with this, that everyone will laugh.

Discovering a Theme

All plays, even those that come about as the result of improv, have a theme. That is, they mean something beyond just the words or characters or actions. The theme of some of the exercises in Chapter One has to do with learning to get along with others. Or put another way: Everyone needs to learn to compromise in order to get along.

For instance, how did you solve the problem posed when one friend buys another a vanilla ice cream cone which the second person detests? If you brought this to a satisfactory ending and still tried to maintain the friendship, you needed to compromise.

On the other hand, if, for some reason — which isn't too likely in the situation with the vanilla ice cream — you decided to end the relationship, there would be another theme. Perhaps it would be: Little things often cause the breakup of relationships. Or even: Little things often act as the straws that break the camel's back. In other words, in some friendships, there may be a lot of conflict that goes unmentioned but undermines any good ongoing involvement. Maybe you and a long-term friend each has developed new interests or totally different lifestyles. Yet for whatever reason, maybe because you've been friends for so long, you have tried, against all odds, to keep the relationship going. Then something like the situation with ice cream cone comes about, and you see that this is just one sample of your friend's thoughtlessness.

How you interpret each of the basic situations of the exercises in these chapters, goes a long way in determining the theme, or what the piece means.

As you learned, almost anything can be treated either in a serious or humorous way. Decide which you think would be better for the following situations. Also, decide what theme you want to bring out. Then figure out the best way you can do this. For instance, in Exercise 1, the theme could be that cheating is wrong. Or it might be that friends should always help friends. There could be any number of others depending on how you develop the exercise.

21

1. CHARACTER 1: You are extremely dishonest. You keep cheating a friend out of money. Rather than being angry, the friend is concerned that someday you will get into big trouble. In addition to being a cheater, you also are a liar who won't admit that you've done anything wrong.

CHARACTER 2: You and Character 1 have been friends since childhood. For some reason that you can't figure out, your friend has started cheating people whenever an opportunity arises. This friend also lies about it. Although you're becoming very disgusted about all this, you are genuinely worried that something terrible will happen as a result. You do your best both to convince your friend of this and to try to get the person to change. At the same time, you wonder what could be the underlying cause.

Since the setting and the situation are nonspecific, you can invent whatever circumstances you wish. You can start with a specific instance of cheating or lying, or you may just bring it up in conversation while walking home from school or whatever else you decide.

In a class discussion try to think of as many different themes as you can for the last exercise. For instance, an underlying theme might have to do with emotional problems and might be stated: Emotional problems can cause people to do strange things.

Themes often can be stated in the form of adages or old sayings. One such theme here could be: A friend in need is a friend indeed. If you chose this theme over the first one, what might now be different about how you play the scene?

2. CHARACTER 1: You are greedy and refuse to share anything. You and a friend are hiking in the mountains. Your friend needs a drink, but you are the one who is carrying the water.

CHARACTER 2: Your mouth is so dry you can hardly speak; it feels like little balls of cotton have formed on your tongue. Yet your friend refuses to give you a drink.

In this improv, try to determine an underlying reason that Character 1 refuses to share the water. Although this person generally has a streak of greed, this seems to be carrying it to extremes. You also need to figure out, since one of you has such an undesirable trait, how and why the two of you have remained friends.

This makes the exercise somewhat more involved than others you've done to date. Therefore, take a little more time, three or four minutes perhaps, to discuss and plan the scene before presenting it. As you did in Exercise 1, figure out a logical theme or underlying purpose.

The situation is a little more specific in this exercise than in the first one. You at least are given a general type setting, the mountain where you're hiking. But the details are left up to you.

3. CHARACTER 1: You work in a restaurant after school and a few hours on weekends. You get along well with your co-workers, but then you discover that one of them is stealing money. If, for instance, a customer orders a steak dinner, the person who is stealing will mark it down on a duplicate order form as a hamburger but charge the customer for the dinner. Later, the person switches the slips to keep the manager in the dark. The employee then pockets the difference. You aren't sure what to do about this. You like the other person, but stealing is certainly wrong. You decide to confront Character 2.

CHARACTER 2: You are conducting an experiment to see how easy it is to deceive others. You decided to do this for a class project in psychology. You know your teacher wouldn't approve of such a wild plan as yours, so you don't want to say anything about it until the experiment is finished. Then you will repay all the money. You know you're taking a risk, but you want a good grade in psychology, and you think this is an excellent way to get it. When Character 1 confronts you, you are determined not to admit what you are doing, but you have to be able to continue the experiment.

The theme here, as in most situations, goes a long way in determining who is the central character. If it's Character 1, the theme might focus on the person's moral dilemma about what to do. If it's Character 2, the theme could relate to doubts he or she may have about following through with the experiment.

4. CHARACTER 1: You've never had any extra money to buy the things you'd like. You are envious of your best friend, who always seems to be able to buy almost anything or to receive it as a gift from relatives. Your family is going on a weekend camping trip, and you've invited Character 2 to come along. You are a little bit angry that he or she has brought a lot of obviously new camping equipment while your gear is years old. Your friend says how nice it would be to have parents a little more like yours, parents who always do things with their kids.

CHARACTER 2: Although your parents buy you anything you want and give you a big allowance each week, you wish they'd give a little more of themselves. Other than buying you things, they are totally involved with their careers and rarely pay much attention to you. You are envious of your friend whose parents really seem to care about their kids. While on a camping trip together, you tell Character 1 how envious you are.

This exercise is a little different in that both characters have the same trait of envy.

One theme here could be: The grass is always greener on the other side of the fence. What other themes can you come up with that would be logical here?

5. CHARACTER 1: Although you and Character 2 have been friends for years, you strongly dislike the fact that your friend is just plain lazy. When you're together, you have to do everything that needs to be done.

CHARACTER 2: Character 1 always seems to want to be in charge of whatever you do. Long ago, you gave up trying to take the initiative when you two are together. Although you like your friend a lot, you don't like this "take charge" attitude. In fact, it's come to the point where you've given up on even trying to help with anything Character 1 suggests.

Here, of course, we have two characters who look at the situation in entirely different ways. You need to decide what, if anything, you want to do about this. For this exercise, in particular, there can be many different themes. Choose one of these and take a minute or two to plan the improv.

Determining the Whys

From now on, in the scenes involving two people in conflict with each other, no matter how silly or outrageous a character's traits are, try to figure out an underlying motivation for this trait, the "why" behind what the person does. Then whether in actual words or only by implication, show the audience what it is.

The reason behind the action can help make a scene come across more logically. Motivation is similar to — though definitely not the same — as intention, which you will read more about in Chapter Four.

In the following exercises, determine both a theme and a possible motive (or a "why") behind the two characters' actions. Remember that each person who does the scene may figure out a different theme and different motives for each character.

In the first exercise, for instance, the parents' action may be motivated by concern for the teenager's well-being in getting enough rest. In other words, the motive is to see that the person gets adequate rest. The teenager's motive could be to gain the heretofore lacking acceptance by peers.

1. PARENT: You insist that the teenager always be home by ten on school nights. This has always been the rule.

TEENAGER: You are in the school play. Although rehearsal always ends by nine or nine-thirty, most cast members stop off afterward at a fast food restaurant. You want to be able to join them. This would mean that you couldn't be home on some nights until after ten.

2. TEACHER: You want a particular student to represent the school in a citywide speech contest being conducted by a local service club. The subject is "How to Improve Our City."

STUDENT: You just moved to the city last year and miss your old home. You hate the new place, and in your opinion, it's so bad that nothing can be done to improve it.

Along with theme, motive can help determine the way a scene progresses or the way it comes across to an audience. What are

25

two possible motives for the teacher's asking the student to be in the contest? How might you play each of these differently?

3. COACH: You have an ironclad rule that anyone who misses practice cannot play in the next game. The only excuses are illnesses or family emergencies.

STUDENT: You believe that your instance of missing practice qualifies as a family emergency. Your father's oldest and dearest friend was arriving in town, and not only did you have to meet him at the airport but entertain him until your parents came home from work.

If you are the coach, you might play this as if you are completely in the right. Or you may recognize that the student had no choice. How would the character differ from one of these feelings to the other? How would your motive differ? What character traits or feelings would you emphasize if you decided to use the first approach? The second?

In playing the student, you could approach the character as being completely in the right or as knowing deep down that you violated one of the coach's rules. How would your playing of the scene differ from the first of these to the second? What is a logical motive here?

4. OLDER SIBLING: Home from college, you see your sibling running around with the wrong crowd. You know this can only lead to trouble because you went through the same thing. In fact, you got into big trouble once with the police because of this.

TEENAGER: You do not understand where your sibling gets off telling you what to do. It's your life, and you should be able to lead it as you wish. Besides, the Older Sibling is just that, not one of your parents.

Here and in the following exercise — as with many others in the book — you need to set up a confrontational scene. Each scene probably will be much different from any other.

5. GRANDPARENT: You think things in general are too easy for

your grandchild. You think that having to struggle more for what he or she wants is an excellent way to build character. Besides, in your opinion the grandchild is not at all appreciative of all his or her advantages.

TEENAGER: Although you love your grandparent, you think the person is old-fashioned and is operating on outdated principles. If you have advantages the grandparent didn't, so what? That's just the way things are. Besides, you feel you do show appreciation by helping around the house and in baby-sitting your younger siblings for free.

Background, Setting, and Character

So far, except for the last set, the exercises in this chapter have involved two teenagers. The following can be whatever characters you want to make of them. Also, so far, you've been told at least some background information on the characters and occasionally on the setting.

In these exercises, since you are given only two sets of lines, you need to figure out any important background information. You need to decide:

1. Who are the characters?
2. What happened to cause the lines to be spoken?
3. Where should the improv go after the delivery of the opening dialog?
4. The theme.
5. Each character's motivation.

The opening dialog should suggest situations and characters, though what you come up with probably will be different from what anyone else does.

1. CHARACTER 1: Hey! What do you think you're doing?
   CHARACTER 2: What do *you* think I'm doing?

2. CHARACTER 1: You're not leaving till you finish what you started.

     CHARACTER 2: Says who?

3.   CHARACTER 1: When are you going to grow up?
     CHARACTER 2: Look who's talking!

4.   CHARACTER 1: You're not seeing him again, are you?
     CHARACTER 2: So what if I am? It's none of your business.

5.   CHARACTER 1: I hate it when you do that kind of thing!
     CHARACTER 2: I guess you'll just have to live with it, won't
          you?

6.   CHARACTER 1: Get a life, will you!
     CHARACTER 2: What's that supposed to mean?

7.   CHARACTER 1: What on earth's wrong with you today?
     CHARACTER 2: Me? I don't know what you're talking about.

8.   CHARACTER 1: You certainly could have helped me a little
          more. I mean I've always helped you,
          haven't I?
     CHARACTER 2: Not with this sort of thing you haven't!

9.   CHARACTER 1: I never expected this from you!
     CHARACTER 2: Oh, really! What did you expect?

10. CHARACTER 1: Why do you always do that to me!
     CHARACTER 2: Look, man, I told you I was sorry.

Now take the same exercise you did and reverse roles. You can use the same set of circumstances and the same two characters you already established, or you can change them.

11. For this exercise:
    a. Come up with your own sets of opening dialog for three
       or four new scenes.

b. Choose a partner and trade papers with another set of partners.
c. Use one set of dialog you received in the exchange as the basis of a scene.
d. Now take the same set of dialog and establish both different characters and a different set of circumstances.
e. Do all of this with another set of opening lines.

Improv doesn't have to involve two people. It can involve either less or more. The next chapter will begin to explore ways in which improv can be used for presenting monologs.

Chapter Three

Monolog Improvs

Monologs serve a number of purposes. Stand-up comedians' routines most often consist of monologs. One-person shows are made up of monologs. This includes shows in which the character plays a real person, as has been done with such literary figures as Mark Twain, Gertrude Stein and Emily Dickinson, or a fictional character. Or occasionally a performer talks about his or her life.

Performance pieces often contain a series of monologs. Most such presentations involve a single artist who often combines acting, oral interpretation, pantomime and dance with various visual and sound effects. The performers often point out particular themes or social problems, taking a strong stand on certain issues.

Monologs, like other improv pieces, have to have a satisfactory resolution. In most cases, they cannot ramble, unless the performer is rambling for comic effect. Often, just like other improvisations, they contain conflict. Since there is only one performer, any conflict with another character cannot be shown directly except on rare occasions when the other character is to be thought of as imaginary or invisible.

Following are two examples of monologs:

> Bobbie and I were friends. Not girlfriend and boyfriend. Just friends. She played clarinet, and I played trumpet. We always had this competition about who would go to district and all-county band, and who wouldn't.
>
> We knew that when we were seniors, only one of us would go to all-state band. Nearly always seniors were picked, and only one from each school. We each pretended it didn't matter which of

us went. But it mattered a lot.

In spite of that, we did our best to help each other however we could, practicing together, often playing duets at community picnics in the summer and meetings of civic clubs and church groups the rest of the year.

In our senior year, things went bad in the community. The factory shut down. That didn't matter to me so much 'cause my dad didn't work there. Besides all-state band was getting close, and that's all I could think about. One day I decided to drop in at Bobbie's and see if she'd heard anything about who was going. I knew she probably hadn't, but talking about it was important too.

She answered the door, tears in her eyes. Had she heard? Had I been chosen and not her? I couldn't help the feeling I had then, a feeling of victory, of excitement. Then I saw these things spread out all over the living room floor. Books and clothes and boxes. "We're moving," Bobbie said and asked me inside. I couldn't believe it and asked her why she hadn't told me. She said she'd just found out that morning. She started to cry. "I don't want to move," she said. "Not when I'm so close to finishing school here." She said her father was out of work, and there wasn't any job he could get nearby and they were moving ninety miles away.

It was like she'd punched me in the stomach. We were friends. She was my best friend, really, if a boy and a girl can be best friends. Ninety miles might as well have been nine thousand.

Suddenly, she started to laugh and cry at the same time. I asked her what was wrong. "I guess we won't have to worry about which one of us goes to state band now," she said. She broke into sobs and raced upstairs.

I heard Bobbie and her family moved the very next day. I never saw her again. A couple of weeks later Mr. Burcher told me I was going to all-state band. That's nice, I thought. Yet somehow it really wasn't all that important.

As you can see, the boy wants to go to all-state band, and yet Bobbie is his best friend. He's feeling tension and conflict about which of them will go, but when the competition between them is taken away, his being chosen doesn't really matter. The monolog is tied together by the theme of going to state band. It begins with that subject and ends with it. There's a resolution to the problem, though certainly not the sort the boy had in mind.

I love animals. But in the high school where I used to go, everyone hunted. If you didn't hunt, everyone thought you were a sissy. I wasn't going to go hunting that year when I was sixteen, but my dad insisted. So I went along with him even though I didn't want to. We went back along the old dirt road beside the house.

The sun was just coming up over the hill. It was quiet, except for all these birds singing and the crunch of our shoes. We walked past the old strip mine and deep into the woods. Dad said we should split up, that we'd both have a chance that way. I had a shotgun, a 410 gauge, pump action. I stood in a little clearing and waited. The sun rose further, and despite the cold air — it was wintertime — I felt sweat running down my neck.

Suddenly, there was this noise like someone crashing hard through a thicket of brush. I looked up and saw a big buck deer. Almost without thinking, I raised the rifle to my shoulder, aimed, and fired. The deer stopped. For just a moment he stared into my eyes. I was so excited I was shaking.

33

I tried to work the pump action, but I didn't know how. Dad hadn't showed me. The deer turned, leaped over a log and raced off into the woods.

At camp the previous summer I'd earned my Expert Marksman badge. But I'd missed my target. I screamed and yelled in frustration. I was mad at myself for missing. I was mad at Dad for not showing me how to work the shotgun. It was the fever of the moment, buck fever people called it. That was the first time I'd used that gun. The first time and the last. Always before I'd used a rifle.

In a little while Dad came to where I was standing and we walked back home. He'd heard the shot and thought maybe I'd bagged myself a deer. No, I told him, I hadn't.

Like I told you, I love animals — dogs and cats, squirrels, rabbits, horses. You want to know something? I'm glad that deer got away.

As you can see, the boy telling the story feels conflict at first about going hunting. Then he becomes so caught up in the moment that when he misses the deer, he is overwhelmed by anger and frustration. At first he's upset at his dad for insisting he go hunting and then angry at him later for not showing him how to use the shotgun's pump action. Later, of course, he's glad he missed the deer because, as he says twice, he loves animals and really didn't want to go hunting in the first place.

Notice that he drew the monolog to a definite conclusion by tying the ending in with the beginning, showing that despite going hunting, he still loves animals.

Developing Your Own Monologs

The next set of exercises contains ideas for monologs. All involve conflict. (Later in the book there will be exercises to develop other sorts of monologs.) The set that follows suggests conflict but is not specific. That is, they can go any number of directions and involve any number of different problems. What you come up with probably won't even be close to what the next person does. That doesn't matter. All that does is that you figure out what the exercise might be about and how best you can show the conflict you feel because of it.

Skip down and look at Exercise 1. It wouldn't be difficult to imagine that someone might decide that what John did was torture a pet cat. So the monolog might take this sort of direction:

> I hate John. Oh, yeah, well, I know it's wrong to hate. But I can't believe anyone would do anything like that. You want to know what he did? Well, I'll tell you. Just as I was rounding the corner coming home from school yesterday, I saw him with a match, trying to light the fur on Tiger's tail. Tiger's my cat. *(Almost crying)* I've had Tiger practically all my life.
>
> You know what? I noticed things before too. Like once Tiger's paw had a cut and once he had a bloody nose. It was John. I know it was. Wouldn't you hate him too? If he did that to your cat?
>
> And the thing is I don't know what to do. If I don't tell someone what happened — my mom and dad or maybe even the police — it's going to get worse. But I guess I really don't want to get John into trouble.
>
> See, he's already been in a lot of trouble. He's been at juvey — juvenile hall, I mean — three or four times. They even had him locked up for awhile, you know?

On the other hand, you might decide that John has stolen something, has lied about something important, or has let you down in some other way.

Keep in mind that whatever conflict or problem you choose, you need to be convincing.

When planning any of the five exercises, you can begin with the lines that make up each one; you can modify them as was done in the sample, or you don't have to use them at all.

Before you present a monolog based on any of the exercises, it will be easier if you think through what you want to say.

Your monolog will probably be much different from everyone else's, and that's as it should be. No matter how you approach the exercise, it isn't wrong or less worthy than anyone else's so long as you are effective in presenting the character, the circumstances, and a good resolution.

1. I hate John. I know I shouldn't, but I do. I hate him. Maybe you'd hate him too if you saw what he did.

2. I never could get along with Dad. It's a lot worse now, since Mom went up on the hill to live.

3. I overheard her telling her friend, "There must be something wrong with that girl (or boy)." And I realized she was talking about me.

4. The next time I went into town, I decided I was going to confront him (or her). I don't know why he did what he did, but I had to get to the bottom of it.

5. I hate it when my sister (or brother) does something like that. And it's practically a daily occurrence.

Now write out two or three exercises of your own similar to these five. Trade papers with a partner and choose one of the exercises the other person has written and prepare it for presentation.

So far you've learned about theme and motive, and most likely you've already done what comes next. That is, you probably have found an objective or a goal for each of the improvs you've presented.

Finding Your Objective

An objective (sometimes called an intention or a goal) is the point you want to reach after you begin, the high point of the scene. Your intention or goal may be much different from that of any other person doing the same improv and certainly different from the person who opposes you in two-person scenes. Rarely is it as simple as both boys wanting to ask the same girl to the prom, which is an example of both having the same objective. For instance, you are with a friend. You want to go hang out at the mall, but your friend wants to go see a movie.

Even with these different intentions, you have to bring each scene to a resolution of sorts. That's maybe a little easier with two-person scenes than with monologs because you actually can resolve a problem in the scene. In a monolog, it often is a matter of "resolving" the problem simply by deciding on some future action. But then you have to carry through with what you decided — to turn John in for torturing the cat, to speak to him and demand that he stop, to do nothing because you don't want to get him into trouble. At least for the first two choices, you have reached a decision but haven't yet done anything about it.

As you see with the third choice, however, it sometimes is a matter of resolving the conflict in your own mind, even though the problem raised in the improv concerns someone else. This third resolution probably is the least satisfactory because it, in effect, allows John to continue with what he's doing when someone like that obviously will keep on torturing animals.

An objective or goal, when reached, is the high point of the scene. Of course, you may have a resolution different from your own objective and closer to another character's, or you may compromise and resolve a problem satisfactorily but without attaining anyone's original objective. Or you may lose altogether. This, of course, applies to improvs in which more than one person appears, as seen in the following short play, *The Script Writer.* Mel's objective is to find out when his script will air, while the Producer's objective is to keep Mel in the dark.

37

Cast of Characters
Mel, 21-22
The Producer, 40-50
Mr. Fujimora, 35-45
The Announcer, any age

SETTING: The action takes place in a television producer's office in Los Angeles and out on the street where the city is under siege. The office consists simply of a desk and chair.

AT RISE: MEL is in the producer's office, Down Left. The PRODUCER is seated behind his desk while MR. FUJIMORA stands to one side glowering, arms crossed.

MEL: I understand you're the one who will be producing my script.
PRODUCER: That's right.
MEL: I was wondering ...
PRODUCER: Yes?
MEL: When will it be on TV?
PRODUCER: *(Tapping a pencil on his desk in an irritated manner)* Well, Mr. Johns, uh, Melvin, I can't tell you that.
MEL: Hasn't it been scheduled? This is my very first job, and I don't know what to expect.
PRODUCER: You don't understand, Mel. I simply have no way of knowing. Suffice it to say that it will be used when it's most needed. If, in fact, it is needed.
MEL: You told me my scripts were realistic, isn't that right? Realistic and depressing. Just what you wanted. So I don't understand.
PRODUCER: Trust me. Your script is perfect. It shows a heightened sense of reality. Listen to the sounds out there. *(He waves an arm toward the rest of the stage.)*
(There are sound effects of gunfire, klaxons and people shouting.)
PRODUCER: Did you hear? Soon it will get worse. Roving street gangs, gunfire, sirens. People screaming in terror, klaxons, whistles, general pandemonium. Just like your script.
MEL: If you like it so much, surely you must know when —

PRODUCER: Don't rock the boat, kid.

MEL: I just want —

PRODUCER: *(He hits his fist hard onto his desk and jumps up, angrily pushing his chair out of the way.)* Do you see Mr. Fujimora here? He once was a sumo wrestler, and now he's my secretary. He's going to escort you from the office.

MEL: But all I wanted to know —

(MR. FUJIMORA grabs MEL, twists his arm behind his back and gives him the bum's rush Center Stage where the lights come up.)

PRODUCER: That young fellow was good, Mr. Fujimora, but too inquisitive. Oh, certainly we'll use his script. It's one of the best I've seen, except in the good old days. Remember the good old days, Mr. Fujimora? That script about the San Francisco fire. And the one about the Depression. And the one about the War to end all Wars. Ah, well, we have to work with what we have. The new script please. Main character, Melvin Johns.

(The office lights dim, while the main stage lights flash on and off as we hear the sounds of a storm, gunfire, shouting, sirens, screams, klaxons and a sense of general pandemonium. Throughout all of this MEL continues to run first one way and then the other. Then for a moment, the flashing lights stop and there is dead silence as the ANNOUNCER delivers his speech, probably over the sound system.)

ANNOUNCER: Welcome to reality, Melvin Johns. This is your life.

(We hear loud maniacal laughter from THE PRODUCER. MEL again runs from one part of the stage to another at random as the lights and sound effects of pandemonium increase and then quickly fade to black and silence.)

CURTAIN

In this short play, Melvin, the central character, was defeated much more severely that he realized was possible. So, of course, he did not even come close to reaching his objective.

More Ideas for Monologs

The next five exercises are different from the preceding in that opening lines are replaced with background information about the characters and the scene, even though they are fairly nonspecific.

1. Your sibling is always coming into your room and taking your things without asking. You've already had several confrontations about this. Now you're really angry because you can't find your coat, it's very cold, and you have a date in fifteen minutes.

2. You're upset because you asked well in advance to use the family car to drive to an important school function. Now your dad has told you that he forgot and has other plans that are impossible to change.

3. Your best friend was planning to go with you to the concert. You bought the tickets, and your friend has backed out.

4. You have to give up your room to your Aunt Hilda and Uncle Floyd who are coming for a visit. The thing is you can't stand Hilda ever since she embarrassed you in front of friends by remarking that it's too bad you aren't as nice looking as other members of the family.

5. Your English teacher accused you of cheating on the exam. And it's all the fault of the idiot in the next row who asked you to borrow a pen. When you pulled out the extra pen, you forgot that you'd clipped it to two or three folded sheets of paper on which you'd written study notes for the exam.

For homework, come up with your own ideas for two or three similar monologs. Either present one of them yourself or trade papers with someone else and use one of that person's ideas.

Building a Plot

Any story or scene that has conflict begins with what is called an *inciting incident*, the single occurrence that sets off a spark of anger or disagreement. This is where the conflict starts. A character orders the wrong kind of ice cream cone for someone else; a friend refuses to give you water when you need it, or your sibling has gone too far in "borrowing" your coat — if, in fact, he or she actually did borrow it. Tension rises as the two sides confront each other.

The conflict continues to build, to become more intense. The person who needs water becomes angrier and angrier as he tries to get his friend to give him some. This building of conflict is called the rising action because it does rise or intensify as the scene progresses. This in turn causes the suspense to build. Will the person be able to quench his thirst or not? Will the character confront the person who has tortured his cat? Will Mel be able to discover when his script will air?

The suspense and conflict build until it's easy to see that one side or the other will win, or that there is no other resolution to the problem besides compromise. This is called the turning point. It's the place where the character knows whether or not the problem can be solved to his or her satisfaction. The point at which the character wins or loses is the climax, the high point of the scene, which usually ends pretty quickly afterwards.

Most of the time a scene can be more interesting if the audience knows the character's reason for the conflict. Why is it so important to use the family car? How can you convince the teacher you didn't cheat on the exam?

All of these things go to make up what is called a plot, as illustrated in the following.

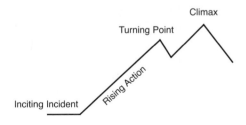

41

Further Reasons for Doing Improv

Did you know that there many other reasons for using improv than simply performance? A few of these are:

1. To help you solve personal problems by talking them out either in a monolog or with others.
2. To put yourself in others' places so you can better understand them and how they view the world.
3. To help others get a better perspective on their problems so that they can solve them.

Let's take the first of these. Although the problems that follow are not necessarily those that you yourself have, they are pretty typical of the types of problems many teenagers face.

These exercises are much more serious than any you've encountered so far, so you can figure out what you think really would be helpful in situations such as these. You may want to talk about them in monologs or play a scene with another character.

After going through the five following exercises in class, you may want to present a problem of your own. For the first time, however, it probably shouldn't be something very serious but something that you do want help with. Your kid brother keeps bothering you every time you want to study, or that obnoxious boy who sits next to you in Spanish class keeps pestering you to go out with him.

On the other hand, if you'd rather not get into personal problems, that's fine. It's entirely up to you whether or not to participate in this kind of exercise or not.

You might keep in mind, though, that it often can be helpful to talk out your problems when you are alone, either as a monolog or by playing two or three characters.

These exercises not only are more serious but they are more specific than many of the others up to this point. With some of them, you may decide to do a scene rather than a monolog. In that case, you and a partner or partners need to choose other characters for the scene and how many of them there will be besides the central character. For instance, in Exercise 3, you may want to choose the girl and her date or maybe the girl and one or both parents.

1. You see a member of your school's most popular clique passing copies of an upcoming exam to his or her friends. You know this to be true since you already took the exam this morning.

2. You caught your little brother drinking an alcoholic beverage. What can you do about it?

3. You are a girl who has been asked to the prom by a boy you like a lot. You said you'd go. The trouble is that he is of a different race than yours. You have no problem with this but your parents do. How can you resolve the problem?

4. You saw a neighbor abusing his small son by hitting him with his fist. You always wondered why the little boy seemed to have so many bruises. You know you have to do something about this, but the father is a well-known member of the community — a politician perhaps or the owner of a popular restaurant.

5. You are with several other teenagers at the home of a friend who is smoking marijuana and insists that you try it. You don't want to, but a couple of the others make fun of you for refusing. What do you do?

If you did the exercises as monologs, now do them as scenes, and vice versa.

Chapter Four

Two-Character Improvs

One of the best ways to learn to understand other people is to try to put yourself in their place and to view the world through their eyes. What would it be like, for instance, to be the old man down the street, the one who walks with a limp and is barely able to see?

The next five exercises can help you to understand others better. They also can help you when you are called upon to play characters that are completely outside your realm of experience.

Experiencing Another Point of View

In preparation for the exercises, choose someone outside of class whom you think is a lot different from the way you are. Then take a few hours after school or on the weekend to pretend to be that person, to try to see the world as he or she might. For instance, if one of the people you choose is handicapped, how do you think this affects their daily life, their general outlook, their treatment by others? From what you can observe, how does this affect the way they feel about themselves? If you choose an older person how does this change the outlook? A younger person?

Try such things as putting yourself in a parent's place. Can you now understand why your mother or father has different views and attitudes toward life than you do? After pretending to be this person, are you better able to understand his or her side in any disagreement with you?

Or choose a homeless person. Try to imagine what about this person or his or her situation brought about a life on the street? What is the person's attitude? Does he or she like the independence of living this way? Is the person unhappy with the situation? Is there maybe a mental problem of some sort that keeps him or her homeless?

Of course, you cannot know beyond a doubt what other people think or feel, but based on what you know about them and your observations of them, you can try to imagine these things.

For an upcoming class, choose someone to try to understand. Then pretend to be that person. Choose something significant about him or her, an attitude or feeling, maybe a strong belief. Then:

a. from that person's point of view present a one- to two-minute monolog that deals with the attitude, feeling, or belief you choose.

b. after you finish the monolog, take a few minutes to tell the class your feelings about the person you chose, what you discovered about him or her, and how the experience has changed your outlook.

Now do the same thing with someone else, but choose the person you know or have seen who you think is most alien to your world or your realm of experience.

In the following, try to put yourself into one of these "alien" characters, a person who is very much different from the way you are. The exercises deal with situations that actually could occur in real life, and so in a manner of speaking are "serious." Most also have their funny sides. When you choose one of the improvs to present, you and your partner can decide whether to try to make the piece serious or humorous.

With any of the exercises, you need to consider all the background that is given. But you are free to add whatever else you want. In Exercise 5, for instance, Character 2 may notice that Character 1 is a former neighbor, an old friend, or an uncle he or she hasn't seen in years.

1. CHARACTER 1: You are someone who is always complaining about physical aches and pains and about life in general. You need to figure out why you do it. You also probably don't even realize that others don't like what you do and often hate to be around you because of it.

CHARACTER 2: You are the very shy person whom you know or have seen in your neighborhood, your place of worship, or anywhere else.

THE SITUATION: Both of you are shopping at the local supermarket. Character 1 drops something, and Character 2 picks it up. The complainer begins complaining! He or she dropped the item due to arthritis or poor circulation or whatever. Character 2 is too shy to explain that he or she needs to get away to keep a doctor's appointment. The shy one continues to become more and more agitated as the complainer drones on and on.

2. CHARACTER 1: You are the nosy next-door neighbor to Character 2, though you prefer to think of yourself merely as interested in what's going on in the neighborhood. You know something is up next door but you don't know what.

CHARACTER 2: Your parents are getting a divorce. You don't want to talk about it to anyone, let alone the nosy neighbor. The reason is that you feel insecure, guilty, ashamed, or worried. Decide which or what combination of feelings you have. Or maybe you feel that if you don't acknowledge the fact that there is a problem, it will go away.

THE SITUATION: Character 1 is on the way home from school when the nosy neighbor calls out and says he (or she) bought a cake he can't possibly finish and thinks Character 2's family might enjoy it. This, of course, is only an excuse to try to pump information out of Character 1.

3. CHARACTER 1: You stand outside and scream at everyone who even sets one foot on your property. You need to figure out why you do this, why it is so important to you.

CHARACTER 2: You know that Character 1 doesn't want anyone to set foot on the property. But you think it's funny to challenge what he or she says.

THE SITUATION: Character 2 often has run across part of Character 1's property just to get the person riled up. He (or she) now does it one more time. But this time is different. Character 1 begins screaming so hysterically that Character 2 is very much alarmed and wants the person to stop.

Of course, there has to be a reason for the screaming, and Character 2 has to have a reason for being so alarmed or worried. As you plan the scene, you need to figure out these underlying reasons.

4. CHARACTER 1: You are blind, so you need to make this handicap come across as true or real. Yet even though you are blind, you don't want anyone ever to give you help. Sometimes, of course, you can't do everything on your own, and this really upsets you. You need to decide why you don't want help, what in your background elicited this sort of reaction from you.

CHARACTER 2: Your parents have sent you to pick up the laundry. Just after you get there, you see Character 1 carrying a bag of laundry and coming into the place. The problem is that everything has been rearranged and remodeled so that Character 1 is having great difficulty navigating the obstacles in his or her path. You have a handicapped parent and are very sympathetic to those who need help.

THE SITUATION: Character 2 offers to help Character 1 who refuses any aid but continues to bump into things. Again, you offer to help.

5. You are homeless, not by your own choice but because you were downsized and haven't been able to get another job. At every place you've applied they've told you that you're overqualified. They won't hire you because they say they're sure that once you have a better offer, you'll leave. This is extremely frustrating since you'd be willing to take almost any job. You're hungry to the point of stomach pains and weakness. You've heard that there are places that offer both food and shelter to the homeless, but you're too new to the streets to know where they are — you never paid attention to this sort of thing when you were working — and now you're too proud to ask. However, you're worried that you may pass out or worse from hunger. You simply have to get something to eat.

CHARACTER 2: You don't like the homeless; you feel they're

shiftless and lazy, that they're parasites who want to live off the kindness and generosity of others. You feel no kindness nor generosity toward them.

THE SITUATION: Character 1 is on street corner that Character 2 is passing. He (or she) gets up enough nerve or determination to ask for help. Character 2 sees what shape the person is in but feels no pity. Then Character 1 faints.

Now do the same improv with the two of you switching roles.

Real-Life Problems

The next set of exercises involves more problems that are like those that many teenagers have. In fact, improvs based on exercises such as these often are used to help people talk out their problems and hopefully gain new insights into them and their possible solutions. You can choose to do the improvs either as monologs or as two- or three-person scenes.

In fact, it might be a good idea to try one of the exercises both ways, that is both as a monolog and as a scene.

1. You are a girl whose parents refuse to allow you to use any makeup, and you feel ugly and out of place.

2. You are a boy who wants to go out for football, but your parents say the sport is too dangerous. The coach is putting pressure on you.

3. The prom is coming up, and a twenty-year-old friend has asked you to go out with him. You want to, but your parents refuse to let you date an older man.

4. You are being pressured into joining a street gang. You don't want to, but are afraid to say no.

5. You always "freeze" when you have to take an English (or any other) exam. Even though you know the material, it's as if you

haven't studied and can't remember anything.

6. One of your best friends is constantly shoplifting. You try to tell him (or her) that it's wrong. You're afraid he will get into trouble and so will you. You know one solution to the problem is simply to drop him as a friend. But you can't. You've been close for years.

7. You hate to take gym class because you've always been embarrassed about the way your body looks.

8. Your parents insist that you do what in your opinion is far too many chores around the house. What with your part-time job, you don't have time for friends or even for studying.

9. Your father is being transferred out of town, and you don't want to leave, particularly since this is your senior year. You want to stay with friends you've known all your life and finish high school with them. You've told your parents that you could stay with your grandma and grandpa, but your mom won't hear of it.

10. Your father constantly makes fun of you saying you'll never amount to anything, that you're dumb, and that you don't apply yourself. You try as hard as you can to please him, but nothing seems to work.

Now try to come up with two or three problems you've heard about or people you know have experienced. Trade papers with a classmate and present a one- to two-minute monolog based on one of the problems.

Given Circumstances

Another name for the background an audience needs to know in order to follow the action is "given circumstances," which deal with the conditions of the characters and the entire world in which they exist.

In any improv that has a plot or conflict, you need to figure out what in the world of the scene, if anything, is different from the audience's world? Where does the action take place? Is there anything the audience needs to know about that location? Is it a busy sidewalk or a deserted apartment building, for instance?

If the scene takes place in another time or location, or in a world different than the one we live in, what are the conditions there? Are the natural laws the same as in our world? When you bring out this sort of thing, you are establishing a frame of reference that the audience will then accept. Once you do this, you cannot change it. If you are giving a monolog, you can, for instance, bring in a magician or an intelligent robot to help solve the problem. On the other hand, if you're doing a scenes that does involve such a robot, you can't then change it so that intelligent robots never existed — unless, perhaps, you've established that powerful magic exists in the world of the scene, and so you can change history however you wish. You need to let the audience know of any important differences or anything important about the characters.

You don't have to give the background information all at once. In fact, it probably would be boring to do that. Rather, you can piece it out little by little, which most likely will also help build suspense and thus keep an audience interested. Be sure also that the information you piece out really is necessary. Rather than stating a lot of things, it's much better to step right into the middle of the action. In the case of a father's being transferred to a job in another town, the audience doesn't need to know what sort of work he does, where the family will live, and so on. (However, it may make the situation more real to mention that he's being transferred to Pittsburgh or Detroit rather than just to "another town," as the more specific the information, the more real the scene will seem.)

An example of piecing out the information can be seen in the excerpt that opens the following play entitled *The Eyes Have It*. Capital letters are used for the given circumstances.

CONSTANCE: I have a secret, Roberta. I'm jus' dyin' to tell ya. I will if ya promise not to reveal it to another livin' soul.

ROBERTA: Why, Constance, honey, you know I wouldn't tell anyone what passes between us.

CONSTANCE: *(Giggling)* I MET A BOY! *[given circumstances]*

ROBERTA: A boy?

CONSTANCE: He's the cutest little old thing you evah did see.

ROBERTA: Oh Constance. I'm so happy fo you. What's his name?

CONSTANCE: EDMUND. EDMUND JONES. *[given circumstances]*

ROBERTA: Don't know as I've eveh heard a name like that. Does he go ta owah school?

CONSTANCE: No. And this is the part you promise you will nevah reveal.

ROBERTA: You know I'd nevah.

CONSTANCE: All right then. HE DOESN'T GO OWAH SCHOOL. HE'S A BLUE! *[given circumstances]*

ROBERTA: *(Gasps and grabs the base of her throat.)* Why Constance Marie Smith, I don't believe I want to be entrusted with that sort of news.

CONSTANCE: Roberta, I'VE KNOWN YOU ALL MY LIFE *[given circumstances]*, and I nevah would have believed —

ROBERTA: There's a place for the greens like us, and a place for the blues. If God had meant us to mix, he would have put us in the verra same school. I do declaah, Constance Marie, I am shocked. Shocked, do you heah?

CONSTANCE: Yes, I do. I do heah, and I'm mightily disappointed. SINCE OWAH BIRTHS, HAVEN'T WE PRACTICALLY SHARED THE SAME CRADLE? THE SAME *(SOBBING)* HOMES ALMOST. *[given circumstances]*

ROBERTA: There is somethin' in what you say, Constance. So I will considah caahfully. Befoah I climb between MY SATIN SHEETS *[given circumstances]*, I will contemplate the mattah and come to a conclusion. But I have to tell you THE VERRA IDEA IS SO ALIEN TO MY BEIN' THAT I CAN'T EVEN IMAGINE IT. *[Background; shows her continuing feelings]*

CONSTANCE: If you met this boy of whom I'm speakin', maybe,

just maybe, you would not have to do any contemplatin'.

ROBERTA: Constance, honey, have I hurt you? I nevah intended such a thing a'tall. I JUS' NEED TIME TO SORT THROUGH WHAT YOU TOLD ME. *[given circumstances; shows what sort of person she is]* I best be goin' on home now. YOU KNOW MY DADDY DOESN'T LIKE ME LINGERIN' ON THE STREET TOO LONG IN CASE ONE OF THEM BLUES COMES INTO THE WRONG PART OF TOWN. *[background, but also meant to be insulting]* Why you nevah know — Oh, Constance, honey, I wasn't thinkin'. I jus' wasn't thinkin'. Fohgive me, say you'll fohgive me.

CONSTANCE: I fohgive you! Ah you happy now?

ROBERTA: *(Sobbing)* I didn't mean it. I didn't.

So far you've been dealing with scenes in which there is a minimum of given circumstances. The following exercises are more detailed. Now you need to be sure the audience grasps the entire situation — the location, the time period, what the characters are like, and so on.

Further, you need to determine the character's intentions. For example, a boy and a girl meet in the school parking lot. It is late at night. One can't stop laughing; the other is simply frightened.

What you need to do is figure out the reasons why both characters are there. What are their intentions, their goals? What has motivated them? Why is one of them laughing, the other frightened?

Maybe the girl has asked the boy to meet her to tell him she can't see him anymore. The other character, who has been her boyfriend, is laughing because he can't believe this is happening. From here, the scene can go a lot of different directions. It can be about a girl whose family says she can't see the boy anymore, and she's sneaked out to meet him and break up. Why? Because of different religious backgrounds? Or because the girl has to get a job to help support her family? Then you need to figure out why the boy finds the situation so humorous. There can be any number of reasons.

Here's another situation:

The location is a street corner of a busy intersection in the downtown section of a big city. A woman is sitting on the sidewalk and won't get up. A man is very angry with her and is trying to get her to move. Maybe:

a. The woman is resisting being taken away by the man, her ex-husband, who has threatened to get even with her for leaving him. The woman's intention is to get away from the man. Her motive is to protect herself from possible violence.

b. The woman is very ill, and her brother had been trying to get her to go to a doctor. She won't, and she also refuses to let him take her there. He insists she get up then and go herself. The woman's intention is to avoid going in for a doctor's appointment. Her motive could be that the doctor her brother wants her to see is a man she doesn't trust due to something that happened in the past.

c. The woman is demonstrating against some cause, and the man is a policeman who is trying to arrest her. The woman's intention then is to bring public attention to the cause. Her motive for demonstrating in public is that she believes strongly enough in the cause to risk arrest.

As you see, the scene depends a lot on intentions. You and a partner need to determine these intentions so you both are playing the same sort of scene.

There are any number of intentions that could apply in all of these instance. Examples are provided for the first five, but for each of these you need to come up with your own interpretation of the scene. After these first exercises, you are completely on your own. You need to determine more given circumstances and the characters' intentions.

1. A high school student is coming down the street and sees his best friend's mother crying. The student tries to talk to her, but the woman shakes her head and says, "Not yet."

Example: The student is coming to see a friend who's been in an accident but doesn't realize the seriousness of the situation. The mother is too overwhelmed with sorrow or grief to talk about it yet. The student, of course, wants to find out how the friend is. The mother becomes upset at the repeated questioning. The student's intention might be: I want to find out how my friend is. The mother's could be: I want to put off talking about this because I am not yet able to deal with the situation.

2. As usual, a teenager cuts across an open lot or field on the way home from school. This time, however, a man wearing a tattered business suit is standing there motionless, pointing to and staring up at the sky.

Example: The man has been robbed and beaten by someone who then took off in a helicopter. The student rushes to him to find out what's wrong. The man assumes that the student was one of those who beat him and has come back again.

Possible intention for the man: I want to get away from this person. For the teenager: I want to help this man.

3. A high school student comes home one day to see a younger sister screaming at the top of her lungs. She doesn't seem to be aware of the older sibling's presence.

Example: The younger of the two characters has just come home and found that his or her bicycle is missing. The other character has to explain that it is his fault. (But you now need to figure out what the older person did.)

Younger sibling's intention: I want my bicycle back.

Older sibling: I want to explain what happened and get my sister (or brother) to calm down.

4. On the way home from work a young woman sees a man in his mid-twenties on the roof of a three-story building. He looks as if he's about to jump off.

Example: The man has been waiting for the young woman, a co-inventor of a quick open parachute. He wanted to demonstrate to her that it really works. However, he accidently dropped it off the roof and into a dumpster filled with old cooking grease from the restaurant on the first floor. The parachute was a model and is the only one in existence. Further, the man is trapped on the roof because the door locked behind him. He wants the woman to help him get down. She's angry at his dropping the parachute and doesn't even want to talk to him.

Man's possible intention: I want to get off the roof.

Woman's possible intention: I want to punish the man for ruining the parachute.

5. A man is kicking the fender of a car in the middle of the street. Another man is trying to pull him away from the car.

Example: The man kicking the fender is the brother of the other man who owns the car and was to take him to an important business meeting. The brother took a wrong turn, and neither could find his way back to the right street. The man now has missed the appointment and is so furious that he jumped out of the car and began to kick it. The brother is trying to calm him down, but he is angry too at the damage being inflicted on his car.

6. The action takes place on a street corner in a foreign country. One person stands on a corner scribbling something on a piece of paper. Another person comes up to him and tries to force him to get into a car.

7. The setting is a high school campus where a student is lying face down and motionless on the lawn. Another student is looking on in horror.

8. Two people are sitting on a park bench acting very nervous. Another person comes along carrying a very heavy box. "Not for love or money," he says, "will I ever do this sort of thing again."

9. A person is sitting at a kitchen table, leaning over, forehead resting on his or her wrists. A second person stands behind the first

one holding a poker from the fireplace high above his or her head.

10. A person stands on a street corner wearing a Halloween mask. It is not Halloween or even close to it. A second person is facing the one in the mask and speaking in a threatening tone.

Depending on the intentions, of course, a scene can go any number of ways. But what if in a two-character scene neither character knew the other's intention. That's exactly the case with the following exercises. Your teacher or a classmate will give you and your partner your intention or objective for the scene without letting your partner know what it is.

Here's an example:

The Situation: A young man is dragging a sofa down a sidewalk. A young woman is sitting on the sofa.

Possibilities:

a. The young man wants to help the girl move to her new house. The young woman is angry with him and doesn't want his help so she sits on the sofa to make it too heavy.

b. The young man wants to get rid of the sofa. It's a family heirloom and the young woman wants to keep it, or the young woman wants to see how strong he is, how much weight he actually can move.

c. The young man and the young woman are making a TV commercial in which the sofa maker wants to show how sturdy the furniture is. The young man's intention is to do a good job with the commercial so the sofa maker will hire him as the company spokesman. The young woman, his ex-girlfriend, is angry at him and wants to make him look as bad as possible.

d. The young man is worried about his wife who won't get up; he is trying to shake her loose. The wife unknowingly upset a jar of epoxy glue on the sofa and then sat down. She's stuck. She wants to keep her husband from realizing what a dumb thing she's done.

Of course, the list could go on and on. In a class discussion, see how many others you can come up with. There are many directions each of the following could take. Do a scene based on these exercises, and then see how different your improv is from anyone else's.

1. The action takes place in a restaurant where a waiter is just bringing someone a steaming plate of food. However, the person who supposedly is being served is getting up to leave.

2. The action takes place in a high school gym. The coach is trying to talk quietly to a student. The student keeps arguing with the coach.

3. The action takes place in the band room of a high school. A student is trying to put a tuba on the floor. The teacher is trying to take it away from the student.

4. Each of two students is holding a woman's hat that is covered with fake flowers and has a veil. Each is trying to yank the hat free from the other's grasp.

5. The action takes place in a social club for men only. Father is there, and then his daughter comes in.

Chapter Five

Improv Rules

What will the rest of the class think of your improv presentations? Be sure to let them talk about what you've done. Often we can't see our own errors or any areas that need improvement. It's often hard to be objective about our own work.

Remember the critiques that you receive are meant to be helpful, not hurtful, and that when you critique what others have done, try to be as constructive and supportive as possible. The critiquing should have to do in large part with if the improv worked, if it came across well. If so, what did the actors do that was good? If it didn't come across well, why didn't it?

You can learn a lot by watching what others do and by critiquing them. You see what they did that was good and what you would like to avoid in the scenes that you present.

Some Important Rules

1. Pay attention and remember. In order for improv scenes to work, particularly those with two or more people, you need to listen to what the other characters say. Don't try to think ahead to what you are going to say in the next seconds or minutes. An improv takes place "right now." If you don't pay attention to the "now" of the scene, more than likely it will fall flat. Remember and use what you have heard and seen to build the scene further. Analyze the meaning behind the words and decide how this affects your character.

2. Once something is said, it becomes a part of the scene. You should not argue with it. In the first exercise that follows, suppose you are playing the farmer. You may have decided that right away you are going to get the car moved with the help of the strongman.

Suddenly, the Person With Amnesia remembers that it's not his or her car but the doctor's, and it has to be returned immediately or the doctor will miss an important surgical procedure he plans to conduct.

As the Farmer, you knew nothing about this. But now it becomes a "fact." It has to be incorporated into the scene. You can't say something like, "That's not true. What really is happening is that the Strongman and I are going to move the car." That or anything similar would destroy everything the three actors have built up to that point. Or suppose you have established in the scene you're playing that there is a car there. You can't suddenly destroy this illusion by saying, "Oh, it's only an imaginary car; anyone can move it." That not only pulls the audience out of the scene but ruins any "reality" that has been established. You have to take what has been established and work from there, even though you wanted the scene to go a different way.

You need to be constantly aware of what is occurring and of when the scene switches directions. Then you have to go along with the change, no matter how "dumb" it seems. In fact, you even have to support this new fact and make it "not dumb" by incorporating it into the show. If the Person With Amnesia starts to talk about his or her childhood or something that happened yesterday, you can support this. Perhaps you can call attention to the fact that the amnesia is "selective," that the person can remember certain things.

3. Don't ask questions that ask the other characters to provide information. Don't, for instance, ask what the Person With Amnesia is now remembering. That puts the actor on the spot and also shifts responsibility from you to that person. If you want to bring this up, add information. For instance, "My brother had amnesia. We let a horse kick him in the head, and it cured him." Then turn to the farmer. "Surely, Mr. Farmer," you say, "you have a horse around." Not only have you contributed a new element and a new direction to the scene, but you've moved the story along. You've incorporated something new into the scene, something you yourself have come up with.

4. In an improv scene, you don't need a lot of exposition. Don't begin by setting the scene: "I'm glad I finally made it home. Wasn't that a terrible storm we had?" That's not only boring, but it's static. Instead, look at your watch and breath a sigh of relief. Shake imaginary rain off an imaginary hat ... or whatever else you can do to suggest any needed background. You can perform these actions while also moving the scene forward by what you say. Don't waste what can be acted out by talking about it.

5. Once you've created an imaginary prop, or when any prop is called for, such as the car in Exercise 1, everyone has to be aware of its placement and size. It can't suddenly shrink or grow bigger. You can't walk through it.

6. If the scene is humorous, let the humor grow out of the situation or the characters. Don't try to make jokes or work to say things that you think will get a laugh. This too will destroy the reality of the scene.

7. Establish your character for each scene. Then act in character and not as yourself. When you establish a specific character, maintain it throughout the scene even when you are not speaking. This means that you need to listen and to react in character.

8. Play every situation in every environment as if it's real — even if you think it's silly or dumb. You and the other characters need to establish your environment for the audience and for each other by what you say and do, but mostly the latter. You "show" that there's a door there in that empty space, or that a big statue stands right in the middle of the living room.

9. Be as specific as possible in what you say and do. Show exactly what you mean. Say that the car is a decrepit Model T Ford, for instance, instead of just a car. Specifics such as this help establish the truth of the scene. They allow both audience and

actor to visualize the action more exactly. They help make it real.

10. If the scene is to have conflict, establish the conflict as soon as possible; otherwise the piece will seem to lack direction. When the characters' balance or routine is upset, the story really begins. (This is the inciting incident, the beginning of the conflict.)

11. Be supportive; help the other actors in the scene. Don't tear down or deny what they do. Remember that improv truly should be ensemble acting. That means that no one in the scene is more important than anyone else; there are no stars. Each piece of dialog and each action should support the overall scene.

12. Keep each scene as simple as possible. There's enough to remember when you have to listen to the other characters without trying to complicate the action.

If you follow these general rules, improv is not difficult. The human mind is logical. It wants to make sense out of chaos. So no matter what the situation or the action, more likely than not you can bring it to a satisfactory conclusion if you only trust yourself and the others in the scene.

Occasionally, you may freeze. It happens to everyone. But the others in a scene are there to support you and get you safely past whatever it was that made you stop cold.

A Few Silly Improvs

The following set of improvs is totally ridiculous and purely for fun, though, of course, you have to make the world in which these exist both logical and consistent. A minimum of given circumstances is included so you have to flesh out the rest, including the setting, the situation, and the characters. For each of these, get together with a partner or partners and spend three or four minutes planning each scene. You may even add characters if you wish.

Try to make each improv last at least a couple of minutes.

1. Time: Early morning
   Place: Lonely country road
   Characters: Person With Amnesia
             Strongman
             Farmer
   Situation: A car has stalled.
   Objectives: The Person With Amnesia wants to see a doctor
             who can cure the problem. Strongman wants to
             get back to the circus. Farmer wants to get the
             car moved so he can drive his tractor past it and
             on down the road to a field he wants to plow.

2. Time: Present
   Place: Railroad station
   Characters: Mother
             Father
             Daughter
   Situation: Mother is leaving.
   Objectives: Mother wants to get away as quickly as
             possible. Father wants to have the mother leave
             as quickly as possible. Daughter wants to be
             able to go on the trip herself and have Mother
             stay home.

3. Time: First century A.D.
   Place: Sidewalk in ancient Rome
   Characters: Roman soldier
             Comic Book Super Hero
   Situation: The two characters are arguing.
   Objectives: Roman Soldier wants to send Super Hero back
             to the future. Super Hero wants to help the
             good guys win the Peloponnesian Wars; he
             doesn't realize he's in the wrong country at the
             wrong time.

4. Time: The Present
   Place: A high school archery range
   Characters: Male Student, expert archer
   Girl in the Moon, Diana the Huntress's cousin
   Situation: Girl in the Moon is talking with the Male Student.
   Objectives: Male Student thinks it's ridiculous that a girl wants to be on the boys' archery team. Girl in the Moon wants to prove to Diana that her shooting is just as good and she should have been named the Huntress.

5. Time: Present
   Place: Living room of a mansion
   Characters: Clown
   Very Tall Woman
   Situation: The clown keeps yelling.
   Objectives: Clown wants Very Tall Woman to get off her stilts so they can get into the clown car and go out to dinner. Very Tall Woman wants desperately for Clown to understand that she's never been on stilts and even had to have the ceilings in the mansion raised to accommodate her height.

   In this example, you need to figure out a way to make the woman's height convincing.

6. Time: Three hundred years in the future
   Place: Space Port
   Characters: High School Teacher
   Two Foot Tall Man
   Situation: Two Foot Tall Man is seated in the waiting area playing classical music on his trombonium.
   Objectives: Teacher, who is waiting for a space shuttle to her new school on the planet Xxyth, wants Two Foot Tall Man to stop playing modern classical music and get back to the only good form of

music ever conceived, Hard Rock. Two Foot Tall Man is determined not to stop until he is given an audition with the symphony orchestra; the conductor is sitting two seats away.

7. Time: Today
   Place: Roof of a building
   Characters: Werewolf
              Grandpa
   Situation: The two characters are in a heated argument.
   Objectives: Werewolf wants to learn to fly like vampires in bat form, so he wants to jump off the building. Grandpa: The Werewolf used to be his best friend and so doesn't want to see him hurt.

8. Time: Midnight
   Place: A ritzy apartment
   Characters: Green Person
              Sales Clerk, in charge of hiring
   Situation: Sales Clerk is interviewing Green Person for a job at a store that stays open twenty-four hours a day.
   Objectives: Green Person has a dual objective, to get a job and to work at night because of the sun's rays turning the person's skin purple during the day. And purple is a color Green Person detests. Sales Clerk, who works the early shift wants to go home and go to bed; she thinks it's ridiculous to have a late night interview.

9. Time: 1990
   Place: At the start of the Weird People Parade
   Characters: Ghost
              World's First Intelligent Robot
   Situation: World's First Intelligent Robot keeps trying to catch Ghost who slips right through his fingers.

Objectives: World's First Intelligent Robot wants his best friend, the Ghost, to be in the parade because he truly is weird. Ghost wants to watch the parade and knows that no one can see him except intelligent robots of which there is only one.

10. Time: 1875
    Place: Public Library
    Characters: Teacher
    　　　　　　Librarian
    　　　　　　Star Athlete
    Situation: Librarian keeps hitting the heels of his or her hands against the shoulders of Teacher, shoving the person backward.
    Objectives: Teacher wants to read a dirty book. Librarian thinks dirty books are too dirty to read and wants to confiscate the book from Teacher. Star Athlete wants to study because secretly he is a bookworm. To accomplish this end he wants the Teacher and Librarian to settle down.

11. Time: School night
    Place: An abandoned house
    Characters: High School Girl
    　　　　　　Street Person
    　　　　　　Two-Hundred-Year-Old Man
    Situation: Two-Hundred-Year-Old Man is crying, and Street Person and High School Girl try to console him.
    Objectives: High School Girl wants to have time alone with Two-Hundred-Year-Old Man because her brother has told her he is their eight-times-great grandfather. Street Person wants the crying to stop and stop now(!) so that he or she can go to sleep. Two-Hundred-Year-Old Man is crying because he's overjoyed at seeing his eight-times-great-granddaughter. He wants desperately to

stop crying so he can talk with her.

12. Time: 6 a.m., Saturday

    Place: A street corner of a big city

    Characters: Talking Gorilla

    Grandma

    Situation: Talking Gorilla keeps asking Grandma out on a date.

    Objectives: Talking Gorilla wants Grandma to go with him to have a banana split. He thinks she's both nicer and maybe even more attractive than any gorillas he's known. In fact, it's love at first sight. Grandma wants to get away from Talking Gorilla while at the same time she recognizes his sincerity and doesn't want to be rude or hurt his feelings.

13. Time: Just before sunrise

    Place: A taxi in the mall

    Characters: Vampire

    Siamese triplets, two of one sex and one of the other

    Situation: The two (well, okay, four) characters are trying to disembark from a taxi. But as usually happens, each of the triplets tries to go first. This blocks the entrance.

    Objectives: Siamese Triplets want simply to coordinate themselves enough to get gracefully out of the taxi. Vampire: The sun will soon be coming up, and so he is frantic to get back to his coffin before he turns to ashes.

14. Time: Seventeenth Century

    Place: The roof of an old castle

    Characters: Mummy

    Person Who Can Fly

    Situation: Mummy keeps staggering around on the roof

67

and almost falling off.

Objectives: Mummy just wants to go back to the dirt bed and sleep due to feeling really ill after drinking all that raspberry punch at the party. Person Who Can Fly wants to help Mummy to go back to the nice dirt bed but doesn't want to catch Mummy if he falls, even though Person Who Can Fly can fly. He's just too tired from flying to the Moon to visit the man there, who is his cousin, to try to catch someone and then carry that person to safety.

The preceding exercises dealt with some strange characters and happenings. Actually, they came from cards on which were written "Time," "Place," "Situation," and "Character." Each set of cards was shuffled. At random one card was pulled from "Time," one from "Place," one from "Situation," and two or three from "Character."

Occasionally, one of the elements was changed to make the suggested improv more "logical." For instance, the exercise at the space port originally was to take place on "a lonely road." But since the action occurs in the future, it seemed more in character with the rest of the elements, that the setting be changed.

Only after all the elements went together to make up a package were the objectives of the characters written.

You can do the same sort of thing. It works well to use three by five inch cards. Make five or ten sets listing "Place," "Situation" and so on. Shuffle each pile and draw one card from each, except you should draw two or three from "Character." You now should have five or ten piles with each of the elements listed. You'll be surprised at how well this works. For each of twenty piles used for the preceding, every single one worked out. A few were eliminated because they didn't mesh with the others. They either were too realistic or too serious.

Different Sorts of Improv

For the rest of the chapter you will be working with two types of improv that are different from anything you've done so far. You already may be familiar with an exercise called the Character Interview. This can be an end in itself or it can lead to a further scene.

Here's what happens. Someone agrees to be "it." Everyone in the class or in an audience can ask questions at random. There are three rules to remember:

a. You cannot plan anything out ahead of time.

b. The person being interviewed cannot answer as self but rather as a character that is emerging.

c. Everything the interviewee says has to be consistent with what has gone before. The person cannot, for example, both like and dislike sports or be both tall and short.

Let the questions and answers flow without interruption. That's what was done with the following, which was started with no preconceived ideas at all about the character, the plot, or the situation.

Q: Who are you?
A: You mean my name?
Q: Well, yeah.
A: It's Jefferson Johnson.
Q: Named for two presidents, eh?
A: People always say that!
Q: Aren't you?
A: I'm not even from your country.
Q: Oh, where are you from?
A: Argentina.
Q: Argentina? With a name like that?
A: Okay, my parents had an imagination. My last name is Lopez.
Q: Where are you now?

A: In my apartment, of course.

Q: Where is it?

A: You act as if you don't know anything about me.

Q: I don't.

A: How is that possible?

Q: I don't know, but tell me.

A: I'm a musician. Just appeared at Carnegie Hall.

Q: What kind of musician?

A: A damned good one! *(Chuckles.)* I know what you mean. I play the clarinet.

Q: How long have you been playing?

A: I don't know. I'm bored with that.

Q: Why are you bored?

A: Short attention span, I guess ... *(Laughs.)* No, it's just that I've been asked that question many times. And it's not all that important.

Q: Really?

A: There are other things to life.

Q: Like what?

A: Fishing, reading, beating friends at competitive games.

Q: You're competitive, are you?

A: *(Laughs.)* You could say that. It always gets me into trouble. I can't turn down a dare.

Q: What kind of dare?

A: Skydiving, tightrope walking.

Q: You've done those things.

A: Yes ... When I was with the circus —

Q: The circus?

A: You must know that! Everyone's heard of The Great Lopez.

Q: Sorry.

A: Trapeze artist. Perfected the quadruple.

Q: You mean spinning head over heels four times! How did you get from that to being a musician?

A: A classical musician!

More often than not, an interesting character emerges. You can try to generate more interest by always asking if the character has any big problems. Still, if you don't like the character you've come up with, try again. It takes little time and effort. When you are being interviewed, it is important to say the first thing that comes into your mind just as you should do in any improv scene. If you become concerned about how your answers will sound, you're defeating the purpose of the exercise.

Let's go back to Señor Lopez. What can we figure out or infer about his character? First, though he says he's from Argentina, he doesn't sound very Hispanic. Could he therefore be lying?

Other things we can determine are that he has "an attitude." That is, he thinks pretty highly of himself and seems not to care who notices. If what he says is true about being both a classical musician and a trapeze artist, he's a very talented and unusual person.

You could go on and on determining traits and attitudes about him. A character interview such as this can be interesting to an audience, though before you agree to do this sort of improv in performance, you probably need to practice several times with classmates.

You also can take the character that has emerged and put him or her in a scene with another character developed in this way. Then have the two characters talk about something suggested in one or both of their backgrounds, but to have conflict try to find something that they probably won't agree on. Or you can come up with a topic to give the two characters, something you're pretty sure will cause conflict. You also can have the character deliver a monolog on a subject suggested in the interview. Señor Lopez, for instance, could talk on life in the circus, his attitudes and beliefs, classical music, the importance of being competitive, and so on.

Here is another short interview done the same way as the first:

Q: Who are you?
A: Don Pedersen
Q: How old are you, Don?
A: Seventeen.
Q: Where do you live?
A: Northeastern Ohio. Near Youngstown.
Q: Are you in school?
A: Graduated last year.
Q: But you're only seventeen.
A: Everyone thinks I'm bright, but I'm not.
Q: Why don't you think you're bright?
A: Not going to college, am I? Working in a fast food place.
Q: Does that make you less intelligent?
A: If I were so doggone smart, I'd have gotten a scholarship, wouldn't I?
Q: But you didn't.
A: Yeah, and I'm really ticked off about it. I mean half my friends got scholarships of one kind or another. And there I was, valedictorian. Then nothing.
Q: So are you just going to spend your life working in a fast food place?
A: Maybe I am. So what?
Q: What do you look like?
A: Six feet, two inches. A hundred and eighty pounds. Blond hair, and a face covered with acne scars.
Q: You're really down on yourself, Don.
A: Wouldn't you be? I mean just like my old man said, I'm not amounting to anything.
Q: You're going to listen to what he said?
A: What choice do I have?

What sorts of things can you infer about Don? Why do you think he has such a low opinion of himself? Obviously, he's bright. He finished high school at least a year early.

Take what you know about him and place him in a scene with Lopez. You might try having them talk about self-esteem since they're at opposite polls in that regard. Another good topic would be self-achievement.

Now develop a couple of characters of your own. Choose one of them and get together with a partner to plan a scene.

Misunderstandings

Another way to provide conflict is through the idea of misunderstandings. A friend thinks you're angry with him because you didn't come over to his house as you usually do. Instead, you had to help your dad repaint the house. You try to explain, but the friend thinks you're only making excuses. No matter what you say, he or she won't believe you. Or you are mistaken for someone else, and the person who sees you won't believe you aren't who she says you are.

Exaggerating the misunderstandings can make them even funnier. The friend says he or she is never going to speak to you again and is going to tell everyone he or she knows what a jerk you are. By this time you're getting angry yourself.

When the exaggeration becomes too extreme to be believed, you can play the scene with a tongue in cheek attitude, as often is done in old-fashioned "mellerdrama" (exaggerated melodramas where the hero is too good and pure to be believed, the heroine too innocent and naive, and the villain too horrible). That is, although you are acting in character, a part of you stands off and laughs at what you're doing and invites the audience to laugh. In other words, you know what you're doing in the scene is ludicrous and you let the audience in on this secret ... even though they certainly already know.

You can do this in a variety of ways, through such gestures outside of the role as shrugging at an unbelievable line or rolling your eyes. You can look at the audience briefly or even wink at them. Such a technique can be useful when doing the following two exercises. This technique, however, is for only highly exaggerated scenes, and you should use it sparingly.

These exercises are much more involved than any improv you've done so far. Because of this, you probably need to do a little more work than usual ahead of time. With the other cast members who will be working with you, take fifteen minutes or more to plan out the scene. Each person in the class can join with three others to present an improv based on the story. The farmer can be a woman as well as a man.

Each of the improvs should take at least four or five minutes.

1. The characters are the farmer, the farmer's daughter, the hero, and the villain. The farmer is late with the mortgage payment because his crops have failed. The villain arrives twirling his moustache and demanding that the farmer sign over the property to him. He spies the farmer's daughter, beautiful and terribly innocent. He says if she will marry him, he won't foreclose on the mortgage. Although she despises the villain, she agrees because she doesn't want to see her father suffer. Just then the hero bursts in. He's always had eyes for the farmer's daughter, but has been too bashful to ask her hand in marriage or even to ask her out. They've only engaged in conversations where both of them were too shy to show the other how they felt, for she feels the very same way. The hero challenges the villain to a fistfight. The villain refuses. He suggests instead that they use dueling pistols which he will provide. "Oh, no," the farmer's daughter cries. She rushes to the hero, throws her arms around him, and pleads with him not to do as the villain suggests. "Oh, gosh, Melanie, darling," he says, "I never knew you felt that way." Instead of listening to her, he is more determined than ever to save the farm whatever way he can. He doesn't know that one of the pistols is defective, the one the villain plans to give him.

2. A woman has a brood of seventeen children. She comes home from her job at the factory to find that her husband has deserted her, or so it seems. What is she going to do? How can she feed the seventeen children, all under the age of sixteen? She can send the older ones off to work, maybe even lie about their age, but

74

she's promised them that they all can finish school, and by that she means elementary, junior high, high school, college, graduate, and even post-graduate school. She doesn't know exactly how she'll do that, but a promise is a promise.

She fires the expensive maid/baby sitter and asks the older kids to baby-sit temporarily while she works a double or triple shift at the factory. They don't have to do the housework, though. She tells them that that would be too much of a burden to place on them.

In the meantime, her poor husband hasn't deserted her. Instead, a group of hoodlums has mistaken him for a man of international renown, possibly an opera singer or a movie star. Though he offers to sing for them — he has a terrible voice — they won't listen. He offers to do a scene or two of improv — he's a terrible actor — but they don't pay attention. He must escape and go back home and help provide for the children even though his part-time jobs never help much. He shovels snow for neighbors but only in the wintertime. He mows a lawn or two but only during warm weather. He does this sort of thing so he won't waste any intellectual energy which he saves for writing the "Greatest American Novel."

How is the mother going to survive working all those shifts? How are the poor older kids going to prepare for college and graduate school and post-graduate school if they have to baby-sit all the time?

How is the father going to escape? Will he be able to convince the international hoodlums that he's not who they think he is? If so, how will he do it?

Decide on how many members of the cast there will be and get together with them to plan out the improv. As with Number 1, begin at the beginning and progress to a satisfactory ending. Several sets of actors can present these same improvs.

Part Two

Improvisational Conflict
with Non-Human Forces

Chapter Six
Situation Improvs

In any improv or play story in which there is conflict, there are a protagonist and an antagonist. The protagonist is the hero or heroine, the person the antagonist opposes. One way to think of this is that the protagonist is the good guy, like the hero in the tale of the man about to lose his farm. The bad guy is the villain, like the one in the same improv.

Yet often there really is no good guy as such and no bad guy, even though there is opposition. The gorilla is the protagonist who wants a date with grandma. That is his goal. Grandma just wants to get away from him but at the same time doesn't want to hurt his feelings. That doesn't make her the bad guy. It just means she has a different objective, even though she is the antagonist.

Conditions As Antagonist

Most often, an improv that has a basic plot, that is, in which there is opposition, is between two people. But this isn't always true. The antagonist doesn't have to be another person. In the scene about the mother of the seventeen kids, the opposition really is a combination of conditions that has complicated the mother's life. The hoodlums who have kidnapped the father might be considered antagonists, but they are only part of the problem. It is the condition of being poor, of having so many kids, of having to work hard and so on that comes together to be the antagonist, the opposition. Clearly, the mother — and maybe to a lesser degree the father — wants her children to have a good life, as evidenced by the mother's not wanting them to work much but to get a good education, and the father's wanting to get back to help provide for them ... even on such a silly basis. So the antagonist is the environment or social conditions.

In this chapter, all the antagonists are forces or conditions rather than individuals. Often with this sort of opposition, it is up to the protagonist to change something within himself or herself rather than to try to change the world. It would be impossible for a person who is the butt of prejudice, for instance, to change everyone's attitudes.

Although most of the improvs in Chapter Five had a humorous twist, those that follow all deal seriously with different sorts of prejudices. In these cases, the antagonist can be thought of as personal conditions.

The exercises suggest monologs. Then the monologs become scenes and are carried further. Those who present each monolog should keep the same characters when participating in the scenes that follow.

The exercises deal with prejudice against such things as being heavy, being thin, being very tall and so on. When you choose one of the exercises for a monolog, you do not have to do the one about tall people if you are tall, or about thin people if you are thin. Rather, it would be a good idea to choose one that is different from the way you are physically. This makes these exercises similar to earlier ones in which you were asked to place yourself in someone else's shoes, to view the world from another person's perspective.

The set of exercises has more than one purpose. It allows you to expand the type of role you play, and it can point out problems people often have about things over which they have little or no control. Maybe the exercises also can help in changing negative attitudes toward such people to positive attitudes.

For the first step in the following exercise, there are hints or samples of the sort of thing you might do. Or if you wish, you can do something entirely different. There also are hints — which you also may use or disregard — on some of the things you might want to include in the exercises.

For each of these exercises, it is up to you to choose the intention and the goal.

All the characters should try to help each other with their problems, as well as helping themselves.

In the sample monolog that follows, there is a lot of conflict, but there is no solution. In your monologs, you can try to come up with solutions, but it's better to have none than one that is unrealistic. There isn't going to be a good witch waving a magic wand to change things, or a diet that allows you to eat everything in sight and still lose weight.

Being Overweight

I hate being ... overweight. I've always hated it. Think what it would be like for you if people called you fatty or tub of lard, or the one I hate most, tub of guts. And people think they're so funny when they do it, other kids, I mean.

But it's not just other kids. I've heard my mom's friends or my dad's saying things like: "It isn't good to allow him (or her) to be so overweight. It's going to have an effect in later life." As if I'm worried about later life ... or could even do anything about it. I mean it's right now that concerns me. So what if I'm ... overweight. No, I won't use substitute words. I'm fat. I know I'm fat. Everyone knows I'm fat.

And that's something else. Why does everyone think they have to point it out to me? Like I said, I know it. Who doesn't know it! Even someone who doesn't see me can hear me coming a mile off. Clumping along, huffing and puffing.

I don't know what to do. I've tried everything. Every kind of diet from eating just bread for a whole week to not eating anything. None of it works. It just makes me sick. Well, okay, maybe some of it would work, but I can't stick to it. I tell myself I won't open the refrigerator, but I do. Late at night, like when everyone else is asleep. When I'm hungry like that, if I could just eat a cracker or maybe a carrot. But not me. I reach for whatever's the worst

81

for my weight — left-over pie, a big fatty hunk of meat. I can't control myself.

Aunt Rachel says it's 'cause I have emotional problems. Yeah, I have emotional problems. I'm hurt and angry all the time because people make fun of me. I know that's not what she means. She said that it must be because I'm lacking in self-esteem that I eat so much; food is a substitute for love or being liked.

"Yeah, Aunt Rachel," I'd like to say. "But which came first, the chicken or the egg? Being a tub of guts or having emotional problems? Who can remember!"

Someone told me I could go to something like Weight Watchers or Jenny Craig or whatever. But I'd feel stupid. In with all those old ladies.

So what am I going to do? Can you help me? Can you give me any ideas? I mean, I'm really desperate. I'd try almost anything. Reminds me of that joke I heard. How can a fat person lose seven ugly pounds? Cut off his head!

I don't mean that! I really don't. But I heard of this fat kid who had a heart attack. Sixteen years old, and he had a heart attack. Maybe I am worried about later. That I'll die young, that I'll have a stroke like my great-grandpa and be a vegetable.

Anyhow, can anyone think of anything that's going to help? Please.

1. You are overweight.
Hints:
a. A brother says that in college people are more accepting; if I study hard and graduate early, I can go to college soon.
b. My whole family's fat.
c. Maybe I'll become a sumo wrestler.

2. You are very tall.
Hints:
a. I got tired of people asking, "How's the air up there?" Now I always say, "Fine. How is it down there around my butt?"
b. People are always asking me if I play basketball.
c. I hate not having a bed that fits my body, and having to stoop when I go through a doorway, and how it's so hard for me to get into and out of a car.

3. You are very thin.
Hints:
a. I don't like being called a bean pole and skinny bones.
b. I can squeeze through lots of places where you can't.
c. I'm slender, not skinny.

4. You are not good at athletics.
Hints:
a. I'm such a klutz. I stumble over things and bump into things.
b. Why are athletics so important anyway!
c. Yeah, well, there are lots of other things I'm good at.

5. Everyone accuses you of being a "brain."
Hints:
a. I hate being called a brain. It's nothing that I did; it's what I was born with.
b. I used to pretend I didn't know the answers in class.
c. You know what? Being smart is going to get me out of a bad environment. Already, I have offers of scholarships.

6. Just because you're into computers, people call you a nerd.
Hints:
a. What's wrong with liking computers? Other people like clothes or cars or whatever.
b. It's not like I spend all day on the computer or anything.
c. My dad's always yelling at me and telling me to get a life.

7. You are not good looking.
Hints:
a. I can't help the way I look.
b. Sometimes I just want to cover my head and keep it covered all day.
c. Sometimes I get really mad. Why can't people just like me for me?

8. You are too good looking.
Hints:
a. Everyone thinks I'm stuck up.
b. I'd change things if I could. I really would! People envy me, and I wish they wouldn't. I just want to fit in.
c. Mom thinks I can become a model.

9. You are not the brightest person in class.
Hints:
a. Maybe I'm not so smart, but I get along. I have a better job than you do.
b. I know my parents are disappointed.
c. Nobody understands how hard I try. And I almost never get above a "C" in any subject.

10. You are too shy.
Hints:
a. I don't like being this way. But it's like I'm afraid to open my mouth or something horrible will come out.
b. When I was a little kid, my mom and dad never let me answer questions from other people. If someone asked if I wanted to go to the park or something like that, my parents would say, "Oh, she (or he) doesn't want to waste time on something like that."
c. If I could start over at a new school, I'd be different. It's like everyone here expects me to be the way I am.

Now try to come up with other problems similar to these. Write them on separate slips of paper which the teacher will collect and place in a hat or a box. Each of you now should draw a slip of paper — not your own — and prepare another short monolog about this problem. It doesn't matter if several people come up with the same thing. Each monolog will be entirely different anyhow.

You also can treat prejudices with humor, which often can diffuse dangerous situations. Besides, making fun of something or treating it in a humorous way can make it seem ridiculous and thus help change the way people think about it.

Although the problems are silly, they symbolize real life situations. Such problems often arise out of what is called ethnocentricity. This is similar to egocentricity, people's being totally wrapped up in themselves to the point of thinking they are better than anyone else. The same thing can happen with a group. One ethnic or racial group thinks it's better than any others. And so they begin to think of the others as worthless. And since the group doesn't know very much about them, maybe they even are to be feared. And if something inspires fear in us, it quickly becomes a hateful thing. This is what happens with prejudice against groups of people.

Of course, the same sort of feeling inspired by ethnocentricity can be good. It can account for school or community spirit. Yet fights often break out among people from different schools, particularly at sporting events, which means this good sense of belonging has come to the point where people from other places are bad. Such an attitude, of course, is silly, which suggests another reason for using humor.

1. CHARACTER 1: You have two heads, both of which insist on talking at the same time and saying exactly the same thing. You want to try to convince someone that you're just as good as anyone else, that the old saying really is true: Two heads are better than one.

CHARACTER 2: You don't have strong feelings one way or the

other about two-headed people. You're willing to be convinced that they are pretty much like everyone else, but you do need proof. You aren't just going to accept somebody's word about it.

2. CHARACTER 1: You are absolutely normal, as normal as anyone ever could be. That's the problem; you're too normal. There's nothing else wrong with you, but people seem to dislike you for what you are. You can't understand this since you are ... well, very, very normal!

CHARACTER 2: You dislike Character 1 without knowing why. After all, the person is normal in all respects. Character 1 doesn't understand your dislike or prejudice and wants you to explain it. Since you don't understand it, you try to tell yourself as well as the other person why you dislike him or her.

3. CHARACTER 1: You are a boy-girl (or a girl-boy, which is slightly different). You can't help what you are; you keep changing from one sex to the other, as quickly as from one second to the next or as slowly as once a month. This is very confusing since you and others like you take boys' gym for awhile and then girls' gym and so on.

CHARACTER 2: You hate boy-girls. They aren't natural; they go against the teachings and morality of all that's good and right ... or so you've been told. Actually, you think Chris is a pretty good guy ... er, uh, girl. The problem is you're ashamed to be with "it" for fear of others thinking that you may be a boy-girl too or might become one. Now you and the boy-girl have been assigned to work on the very same scene in improv class. What do you do about it?

4. CHARACTER 1: You are from Mars; that means you're green and have a pointy head. And talk about problems, you speak through your nose instead of your mouth which everyone on Mars knows is solely for eating ... and weeding the garden. Your father was named ambassador to earth and the whole family had to move here. You're the only Martian in your school and desperately want to make friends. At first, everyone was afraid of you. Now they

either stay away or tease you all the time for what you are. You're very lonely.

CHARACTER 2: You secretly admire the Martian. You think the person is very, very attractive since the Martian's shade of green is your very favorite. You also think it's kind of cute that the Martian speaks through his nose. Actually, you'd like to go out on a date with the Martian, but everyone you know advises you against it. You really don't understand why. Still, this is your own life, and you should do what you wish. So one day in the cafeteria, you carry your tray to the table where the Martian sits all alone.

5. CHARACTER 1: You hate Character 2 because his or her mouth curls up on the left side and down on the right while yours curls up on the right side and down on the left. Because of this you know that the two of you are entirely different. In fact, your two "species" have been enemies for years. Therefore you are completely thrown by what Character 2 does.

CHARACTER 2: You know because of the mouth thing that your people and Character 1's have been enemies since the beginning of time. However, you think this is stupid and want to try to change it. You know you can't change the world at large, but on the other hand, one person really can make a difference.

One day you see Character 1 hurrying along toward school — in all probability trying to get away from you — but you hurry to catch up. "Hi," you say, "I think it's silly that we supposedly dislike each other, and I want to change things."

See if you can come up with any further exercises similar to the preceding five. Here are some ideas that might get you started thinking:

1. A person excels in sports, but most people look down on sports.

2. Two separate religions argue over who is right. Each group thinks the other is made up of blasphemers or worse. The thing is, the people of both religions actually worship the same Deity. They

just call God by different names.

3. Someone has a very special talent, such as being able to predict the future. Many people are jealous, and the jealousy changes to prejudice or looking down on the person. In fact, some of the others want to beat up Character 1. Of course, the one with talent to read minds knows what is planned and what everyone else thinks.

4. A person is raised to god or goddess status just because he can charm birds and animals. When this person has no other special talents and can't help the people attain all their goals, they become angry and want to kill the person.

5. Everyone looks down upon one high school student because the person has parents of only three sexes instead of the usual four. In fact, a few other students decide they are going to "teach (the character) a lesson."

You can use the foregoing as the basis for developing other exercises or come up with your own ideas which you then present in class with the help of a partner or partners.

Chapter Seven
Condition Improvs

Try to determine the protagonist and the antagonist in each of the following. The answers appear at the end of the chapter.

Present a scene or monolog or both based on the characters and the situations in the following exercises.

1. CHARACTER 1: You've received a bad grade on an exam and can't play in the next basketball game. You try to see if you can do extra work or do anything else to raise the grade.

CHARACTER 2: You are the coach and are disgusted at Character 1 for messing up. The person has the ability to do good work but obviously didn't study. Still, you need him or her to play in the big game.

CHARACTER 3: You are the teacher who graded the exam on which Character 1 got a poor mark. You know the person is bright, and you've decided to teach him or her a lesson. Being a star athlete does not guarantee good grades, and you're determined to bring that point home.

ACTION: The coach and the athlete have asked to meet with the teacher to see if he or she will allow the student somehow to raise the grade.

2. CHARACTER 1: You promised to stop in at your friend's house no matter what. You share birthdays and have always gotten together to celebrate. The problem is the friend lives at the top of a steep hill and snow and sleet have made the road too slippery for your car to make it. To make matters worse, you'll be moving next week to a town about fifty miles away, and this may be your last chance to get together for a long time.

CHARACTER 2: You have been looking forward to seeing your friend to celebrate your joint birthdays. The person is late, and you look out over the balcony to see if you can spy his or her car. You see your friend apparently stranded about halfway up the hill. What do you do?

Intention for both characters: You want very much to get together to celebrate your birthdays.

What can you do? Present a scene that shows how you either solved the problem or were defeated by it.

3. CHARACTER 1: You sponsored a person for student council president and based the campaign on the student's total honesty. This morning's paper has a story about the person's being arrested with two others for burglarizing a house. You can't believe it! The final campaign speeches are scheduled for today, and you are embarrassed and nervous about facing everyone at the assembly where they will be given.

CHARACTER 2: You've been arrested along with two of your friends for breaking into a house and attempting to rob the occupants. You didn't do it, but nobody seems to believe you. What happened is that you came across a burglary in progress and tried to run off the robbers. You were successful, but then the police came and arrested you.

a. CHARACTER 1: Present a monolog in which you have to explain why you are withdrawing your candidate's name from the ballot.

b. Have a confrontational scene with the candidate and ask what is going on.

c. CHARACTER 2: You should appear before the assembly to present a talk in which you try to explain what happened. Some students believe the explanation, but many do not. Your need is to convince them that what you say is true because you truly are committed to your candidacy.

4. CHARACTER 1: Your watch stopped, and you didn't realize that you were an hour late bringing the car home. You have been able to use the car whenever your parents don't need it. Your dad has said, however, that if you ever violate your curfew, you cannot

borrow it again. You're sure that your dad will understand, and it will be okay.

CHARACTER 2: You are the father. When Character 1 doesn't come home on time, you are worried. This isn't at all like your child who really is pretty responsible. You become so worried that you're going to call the police to see if there was an accident when Character 1 drives up. You're angry and don't want to give your son or daughter the chance to explain what happened. The anger is so intense, of course, because you were extremely worried.

ACTION: The two characters have a confrontation just inside the front door.

5. CHARACTER 1: You and Character 2, your best friend, have known each other since you were young kids. You get along very well, except that for some reason your friend feels the need to be perfect in absolutely everything, no matter what the situation. Now Character 2 has had the last English paper returned. In red ink at the top is a big red "C," the lowest grade your friend has ever received.

CHARACTER 2: For whatever reason, you are completely down on yourself if you feel you've failed. You have to be the best in everything, even in things you're attempting for the first time. Even though you know intellectually that these expectations or needs are wrong and that ultimately it doesn't matter if you're tops at absolutely everything, you can't help the way you feel. Maybe it's because of the pressure you always experience from your family, combined with the fact that your older siblings are highly successful, and deep down inside, you are sure you can't measure up.

Anyhow, you are devastated about receiving the C grade. You feel as if you can't show your face at school anymore.

ACTION: Character 1 drops in at Character 2's house and learns what has happened. Character 2 explains that he or she feels worthless and that maybe life isn't of any value anymore. Character 1 can't understand such an intense feeling but wants to help even though Character 2 doesn't want to listen to reason. Yet Character 1 won't give up in trying to get through to the friend.

The Way Things Are

Just as we cannot change many things about our appearance nor about our heritage, there are certain natural laws of the universe that cannot be changed. The sun rises in the east and sets in the west. Water runs downhill. There are rainstorms and in many parts of the country snowstorms. We may be affected by such things, but we can do nothing to change them.

Even human-made laws most often cannot be changed by a single individual. Although you wish the speed limit were higher or lower, you probably have to accept that it is the way it is. The same applies to rules and regulations at school and even at home.

The remaining exercises in this chapter are similar to the preceding ones in that the antagonist is not a living being but is laws or rules of one sort of another. Therefore to win in a struggle against them, we often have to change something about ourselves. This can be as simple as deciding to live with the rules or as involved as moving to a new location.

Although the exercises in themselves are silly, they are poking fun at real situations that are similar. The first, for instance, isn't really about tricycles but about teenagers driving cars. Sometimes, the problem presented is just the opposite of the real problem, as in Exercise 6 in which the usual complaint is having too much to do around the house.

The intention should be fairly easy to determine. For instance, in Exercise 4, the thirty-year-old student wants to be able to date at an earlier age. The parents won't allow it since they feel the student definitely is not yet mature enough to handle any romantic involvement or relationship.

Laws, Rules, and Regulations

Family Rules

1. CHARACTER 1: You have been assigned a topic in speech class and want to gather information. The topic is Teenage Drivers. You feel that the current age of eighteen in your state for operating a tricycle is much too high. Why in some states, one of your parents says, it's even older. It turns out that this is only one state, however! In some places a child of four can legally operate a tricycle but only at home or on a sidewalk out front. You certainly feel old enough and responsible enough to be allowed to have a license. And you're really tired of the same old story about the tricycle accident Dad was involved in, and the fact that Mom didn't get her license until she was much older. You think all of this is old-fashioned and out of date.

CHARACTERS 2 and 3: You are the parents of Character 1 and are very much overprotective, but then again you hate to see any harm come to your child. Dad brings up — as he always does — an accident he was involved with when he was learning to ride a tricycle. He was four years old at the time and decided to see if he could ride his tricycle down the front porch steps. He couldn't, and the result was a broken tricycle that required costly repairs and a badly cut chin that required many stitches. No matter how many times Dad tells the story, Mom is horrified. She brings up the fact that it never even occurred to her to get a tricycle driver's license until well into her twenties.

2. CHARACTER 1: You are a high school girl who is ashamed to show her face (really her legs) in school, and with good reason. Your parents insist that you wear short skirts, what they refer to as midis and minis, which had something to do with what Mom herself wore back in the "Dark Ages."

The current style is to wear ankle-length dresses or even those that drag on the ground. You can see the point of not wearing dresses that drag because they become filthy and worn and people,

93

both girls and boys, stumble over them constantly. Nevertheless, you are terribly ashamed of having to wear shorter skirts and constantly try to hide your legs, crossing them, sticking them as far back under your seat as you can or whatever. It's always a nightmare to walk to and from school or to change classes, though you must admit that most of your friends are understanding. They know it's your parents' fault for what you wear. But then again a group of older girls always points and giggles when they see you in the hallway.

You simply cannot understand your parents' attitudes.

CHARACTER 2: You are the mother and are totally against long dresses. As your daughter says, they are filthy and easily worn out. But that is not the real issue! The real issue is that long skirts are immoral. They leave things to the imagination that should not be left there. You're determined not to give an inch in this argument that seems to come up almost every day.

3. CHARACTER 1: All your friends are allowed to stay out till 5 a.m. on school nights and 7 a.m. on weekends. You have to be home by 3 a.m. and 4 a.m. respectively. You think this is highly unfair since it isn't just one of your friends who's allowed to do this but practically all of them. You feel that if you have to be home so early, you just don't have time for fun and, as you told your mom and dad, for being a teenager.

CHARACTER 2: You are Character 1's mom. Back in the old days, you say, before the development of those pills that made sleep obsolete, high school students were lucky if they could stay out past nine or so on school nights and past ten or eleven on weekends. You show absolutely no sympathy to the argument that that was the "Middle Ages" and things have changed. Maybe they have, but not so much that teenagers should be allowed to practice total irresponsibility. What with the school day now lasting twelve hours and chores around the house, when does a teenager have time to study except from midnight on?

4. CHARACTER 1: You know that back when your grandparents were young, people began dating when they were fifteen or sixteen and a few girls even married at "sweet sixteen." Sweet sixteen, for heaven's sake! What about "Sweet Thirty-Two." That's when your parents say you're allowed to begin dating. They're very evasive about when they began to date, but you know it was when they were in their early twenties. Uncle Max told you so. At age thirty, you think their rules are terribly unfair, and you want things changed. After all, it is still two more years before you can date, and two years after that till you can even hold hands! That's society's norm, but many of your friends already are dating, some with parents' blessings and some without. You are a good person, however, and don't want to openly defy your parents.

CHARACTERS 2 and 3: You are the parents of Character 1, and yes, you did begin dating in your twenties, but that was before all the recent advances in society and civilization as a whole. That was before all the information began to erupt out of the Information Highway, before longevity pills, and before schools required attendance to the age of thirty-one, making twenty-six grades in all, not counting kindergarten.

You've heard all the arguments, but Character 1 is still a baby in your eyes. Sure, you dated and even married much earlier, but you had to wait longer than your parents. Besides the new enhanced brains do not have anything to do with emotional security, only with the intellectual thinking process. Yes, today's students are much, much more immature and unprepared to face the world of romance and whirlwind courtships than was the norm in your time.

5. CHARACTER 1: You desperately want to be able to help your mother and father around the house. All your friends do chores, why don't you have the right to do them? Otherwise, how will you learn to repair a broken window or stain a bookcase or wash dishes or cook a simple meal? It's unfair; that's what it is.

CHARACTER 2: You want your children to have a carefree life until it is time for them to take on the responsibilities of adulthood.

You can't understand why Character 1 resists this so much. You would have given anything to be free to have fun and to be with friends and not have to worry about chores like you did. After all, you milked the cows, plowed and sowed the fields, harvested the crops, swept and scrubbed the house, dusted, made meals and still had to go to school. You decided long ago that no child of yours would ever have to undergo such a thing.

School Rules

1. CHARACTERS 1 and 2: You both hate the school dress code. Who ever heard of wearing plum-colored bikinis with green trim anyway! You wonder where such a nitwit idea came from and hope to get all the other students involved in a strike or a protest to have things changed. Nobody at other schools has to wear such things. Heavens, no! Their bikinis are striped or speckled or covered with dots or stars, not the drab kind of thing you wear. Why do you have to live in such an old-fashioned place as this anyhow. It's almost as bad here as the place you read about in social studies class, some little town in the northeast where the boys all wear old-fashioned swimming trunks and the girls one-piece swim suits. You remember that your class didn't even know what those things were till your teacher helped you look them up on the Internet. You think you can get the other students behind you today at the rally. At least the two of you are going to try your best.

2. CHARACTER 1: You think it's terribly unreasonable that you can't be more than three months late with a homework assignment. If you are, the teachers will lower your grade one letter and continue to do so for every month you're late after that. That means that if you go the least bit past the deadline, you could fail. Then how would your parents feel? What would happen to all the plans you have for college?
CHARACTER 2: You are a teacher in your second year of teaching. During your first year at the school, you were sympathetic to students' feelings about homework. But then you

started to get all these old papers months after you assigned them. In many cases you couldn't even remember what the assignment had been! That doesn't even take into consideration the extra work you have to do with the grading system, changing F's to C's or D's to B's and A's long after the semester has ended and when you barely remembered many of the students. When Character 1 comes in search of a sympathetic ear, you simply have to nip things in the bud. Even so, this is one of your favorite students — bright with a great personality. In fact, this student is an all-around good kid except for the homework thing. So you don't want to come on strong with your arguments, and you are determined to be fair and listen.

3. CHARACTER 1: You think it's highly unreasonable for the coach to insist that you and your teammates are in bed by 4 p.m. each day. That hardly gives you time to practice with the team, to do your chores around the house, and then do your homework. Your grades are slipping, and you feel so weighted down and dopey from so much sleep that you have a hard time paying attention in class. You simply have to confront the coach about changing the requirements. If you get enough of your teammates behind you, maybe you'll just all threaten to quit the team, and then the coach will see what happens. You really don't want to do that though, since you love the game so much.

CHARACTER 2: As the coach, you want your team to have adequate rest, and if that means insisting on their being in bed by four each afternoon on weekdays and four-fifteen on weekends, so be it. So they miss a little time with their friends or they miss a little TV, later on in life they'll thank you.

After all, didn't Ben Franklin say: Early to bed, early to rise makes a girl or boy healthy and wise! Or something like that. Well, if that was good enough for old Ben, it was good enough for the team. No matter who comes to see you or what the person says, you won't budge an inch. If they don't want to obey the rules, they're off the team. Except then what would you do? You'd be out of a job. Besides, you love the game, as well as liking the salary you receive for coaching.

Views and Opinions

1. CHARACTER 1: You believe that if you're old enough to drive a car, you're old enough to vote. You know that in some states sixteen-year-olds are not yet allowed to drive, but you are. You've been driving more than six months and haven't had an accident. You'd be just as responsible a voter. Besides, if you got the vote for sixteen-year-olds you could launch a campaign to give those your age the right to drive, no matter where they live. You don't know exactly how you'd change the law since the driving age is determined by each individual state and not the federal government. Still, you'd do it.

CHARACTER 2: You are a high school teacher who feels that the majority of high school students don't know a Democrat from a Plutocrat and couldn't care less. When Character 1 talks to you about voting rights, it's all you can do not to laugh in the person's face. Character 1 challenges you to prove that sixteen-year-olds aren't informed enough to vote. You challenge the student to prove that they are.

2. CHARACTER 1: You are going to college in the fall. You plan to work part-time, and you have a small scholarship. Your parents agree to provide the rest of the money you will need, but there's a catch. In order for them to help you through school, they insist that you major in theatre. They both have acted in community theatre and semi-professional productions and are certain you have the talent to be a big star. After all, you did play a supporting role in that junior high play. They know you've been too busy since then to audition for shows, but they certainly recognize talent when they see it ... or so they say.

You don't want to major in dramatic arts. You don't even like very much to see plays, and you certainly don't want to be in them. You think theatre is a waste of time. What you want to do is major in business and then go on for your MBA (master's degree in business administration). After that, you want to open your own business. You can't think of anything more rewarding or even more glamorous.

98

CHARACTER 2: You are the father of Character 1 whom you think is simply being obstinate in not wanting to major in theatre. You wish you had done so, but you didn't have the sense to do it. You know if you had that now you'd be on Broadway or up there on the silver screen. People have accused you of wanting to live life vicariously, that is, through the future theatrical achievements of Character 1. But that's not the case at all ... is it?

Besides, since you and your wife will be providing most of the money for Character 1's schooling, shouldn't you have a right to say how that money is used?

The Environment

1. CHARACTER 1: There's a terrible blizzard but you promised Little Red Riding Hood's grandma that you'd go into the woods and check on the girl. This is because there are terrible stories abounding about the horrible things the wolf has been doing lately. And you're absolutely certain he's trapped Little Red in her house. She means a lot to you; you've known each other practically from birth.

You set out, but you can hardly see in the driving snow. You barely know which way to turn. What are you going to do? In a monolog, tell the audience your feelings, what you have planned, and how you're going to get through all of this.

2. CHARACTER 1: You've met Mother Nature and know that generally she's not an unreasonable woman, except when she's in one of her moods. But you hate rain, and you think maybe if you talk to her nicely, she'll not let it fall anymore.

CHARACTER 2: You are Mother Nature or Earth Mother or whatever people want to call you. It doesn't matter so long as you're in charge. That's very important to you, but it's also important to be thoughtful and kind whenever these two things are called for. Trouble is, you do have these moods. You've been to a couple of witch doctors, a psychiatrist or two and a 1960s blues musician. None of them helped you. And when you get into this sort of mood, you're unshakable in the havoc you wreak.

Besides, people do need rain. Where else would they get water to bathe in, to swim in and to use in espresso coffee? You've known Character 1 since the person was a little baby — you and the person's mother were college classmates — and you'd like to fulfill Character 1's request. But there's the need for rain, and there are your moods.

3. CHARACTER 1: You and Character 2 like to go exploring, to take long hikes and to spend weekends out in nature. This weekend you've decided to go exploring where you've never gone before. You get lost; no matter how determined you are to find your way out, you keep going in circles.

CHARACTER 2: You like to spend the weekends adventuring with Character 1. But this time you're really angry. You're lost, and it certainly isn't your fault. It's Character 1's. Why do you say this? Because it's not your backyard where you're lost. It's among the underbrush and thickets in Character 1's backyard.

BOTH CHARACTERS: You know you aren't very far from civilization; you even hear traffic sounds and the squeals of young children at play. Do you also hear the voice of Character 1's mother? Maybe, though it's hard to tell. Night is coming, and you are going to be stuck here with all the wild things if you can't figure out what to do.

4. CHARACTER 1: You're crossing the desert. You also have just received a new trench coat for your birthday. You love it, but it's very, very hot. You could leave it, but it was given to you by that very special person in your life. But why on earth did the person insist that you to bring it with you to the desert? That's insane.

There has to be a solution. It's up to you to discover what it is and in a monolog to tell the audience.

Now try to come up with some two-person exercises of your own that pit a human being against a foe that is a condition of society, the environment, or nature. Once you have done so, choose a partner and present the scene.

The problems can be either silly or serious.

This chapter ends the concentration on establishing conflict as the basis of improv. There are many other types of improv that can hold an audience's attention.

In the next few chapters you will be dealing with some of the other types.

There was no human antagonist in any of the opening exercises in this chapter. The antagonists for the first five improvs are:

1. The student's own mental state which caused the person not to study.

2. Weather conditions which kept the character from driving the car up the hill.

3. Circumstances or coincidences in the characters' coming upon a burglary scene at just the wrong time.

4. Fate that caused the watch to stop.

5. The mental condition or pressure that forced Character 2 to feel the need to be best.

Part Three

Body Position, Opening
Line, and Object Improvs

Chapter Eight

Body Language Improvs

Not only can situations suggest improvisations, but so can a lot of other things. Some of these are physical placement and body language.

Following is a list of various body positions.

a. Legs spread, arms raised and apart so that you look something like the letter X.

b. Stand with your body open to the class, but with your head turned to the right and your left arm held straight out at the side, palm up.

c. Stand straight, arms at your side with your head to one side resting on your shoulder.

d. Stand with your arms folded in front of you, your feet with the toes pointed inward.

e. Stand with your hands on opposite shoulders, mouth in a grimace.

f. Look straight ahead with both arms stretched out as far as possible toward your left side.

g. Sit in a chair with your arms straight out in front of you.

h. Sit in a chair with one leg stretched out in front, one pulled back and your hands at your sides.

i. Sit with your arms stretched out in front, palms down.

j. Stand with one hand on your hip, the other raised at the elbow.

k. Sit with your hands covering your face and look out in front between your fingers.

l. Stand with one hand raised at the elbow and clenched into a fist.

m. Sit with one hand on top of your head and the other on your hip.

n. Sit with both hands on your chest and your spine arched.

o. Sit with both hands clasped behind your back and your head raised.

p. Clasp your hands together, palms outward, in front of your mouth.

q. Kneel with your arms stretched out at either side, your palms upward.

r. Kneel, arms stretched over your head, palms outward.

s. Bend your arms at the elbows and clench your fists.

t. Sit down, hunch over and let your arms hang between your legs.

u. Bend over backwards as far as you can letting your arms hang loosely at your sides.

v. Stand on one leg, the other leg bent back at the knee.

w. Sit with your index fingers in your ears.

x. Sit with your arms and legs stretched out in front of you.

1. Think of a logical reason for being in any of these positions, a reason that has to do with a continuing action. Now follow through with that action. For instance, the X position might suggest doing jumping jacks, or the position suggested in Letter G might suggest driving a car or typing.

Each person should do at least four or five of these. Try to do something different from what anyone else has done.

2. Work with a partner. You will place the person in a beginning position and a closing position, both taken from the above list. The idea is for your partner to find a logical reason for going from the first position to the second. For instance, Letter H could indicate that the person who assumes it is about to get out a chair. Letter J could suggest getting ready to knock on a door. What you can do then is:

a. Rise from the chair;

b. Get ready to go out;

c. Walk outside and go down the steps and then on up the street;

d. Stop and knock on someone's door.

Switch around so that the partner who assumed the two positions now places the other one in an opening and closing position.

3. Work with a partner. Choose two of the positions on the list. Each of you will assume one of these. Try to think of a logical reason for someone to be in each of them. What were they doing that they ended up this way, and how will they carry through on the action? For instance, if you chose Letter D and Letter F in the preceding list, Letter F could be demonstrating how to do the hula. The other person's position could show embarrassment. A follow through would be for the demonstrator to insist that the other person try to perform the hula, maybe even helping with arm positions and so on.

In other words from the two different positions work together to tell a story.

4. Repeat Exercise 3 with your partner except that each of you should assume a position without telling the other which one it is. Only after you're in front of the class can you try to figure out what the positions could mean for the two of you and how you can work together to tell a story.

5. This begins the same way as Exercise 4. However, as soon as it is clear what the two of you are doing, your teacher will say "freeze." Stop immediately in whatever position you're in. Two new people will assume the positions you were in when the teacher yelled "freeze" and then figure out a new story. Repeat this until everyone in class has had a chance to work with a partner after assuming an old position.

6. Work in threes. One of you should choose one of the following animals to act out in front of the class showing something characteristic about the way it moves or what it does. As soon as one of the others figures out which animal you are imitating, that

107

person should take over after fifteen or twenty seconds. There is a catch, however. The second person still must imitate the animal but in a different way. After another fifteen or twenty seconds, the third person should take over for the second, but with this same catch of imitating the animal differently from the way the other two did it.

For instance, if you decide to imitate a cat, one person could imitate the cat's washing itself, another the cat's rubbing against furniture, and the third the cat's sneaking up on a bug.

Each person in the trio should have a turn being first. That is, after the three of you have imitated one animal, move to a second animal and then to a third. If you'd like, you can come up with entirely different animals from those on the list.

a. a cat
b. an eagle
c. a deer
d. a puppy
e. a fox
f. a hummingbird
g. an elephant
h. a giraffe
i. a lizard
j. a rabbit
k. a squirrel
l. a wolf
m. a coyote
n. a lion
o. a cobra
p. a goldfish
q. a bear
r. a pig
s. a horse
t. a cow

7. Stay in groups of three and do exactly the same exercise except this time pretend to be one of the following insects or one that you come up with on your own.

a. a fly
b. a bumblebee
c. a praying mantis
d. an ant
e. a mosquito
f. a butterfly
g. a moth
h. a dragonfly
i. a caterpillar
j. a cockroach

8. For this exercise, work with a partner. Once again pretend to be something you are not — one of the people on the following list. Do not tell your partner which occupation you've chosen. This time, however, instead of taking over, when your partner discovers what you are doing, he or she should figure out a way to assist you in your work.

For instance, if you choose to be a short order cook, your partner can be a waiter taking what you cook to a customer.

Again, each of you should have a chance to go first. Feel free to come up with additional occupations.

a. a fireman
b. a short order cook
c. a tailor or dressmaker
d. an actor
e. a movie director
f. a sculptor
g. a house painter
h. a bus driver
i. a farmer
j. a writer

k. a newspaper reporter
l. a soda fountain clerk
m. a bagger at a grocery store
n. a detective
o. a race car driver
p. a hair stylist
q. a makeup artist
r. an auto mechanic
s. a cowboy
t. a court judge

9. Now, however, get together with a partner and decide on one of the following activities or another similar activity you choose yourself. Pantomime the activity in front of the class. Keep going a minimum of twenty seconds or even longer if the class has not yet guessed what you're doing.

a. playing tennis
b. playing one-on-one basketball
c. grocery shopping
d. competing in a marathon race
e. doing a scene from an opera
f. hanging a very large picture
g. playing a duet on the piano
h. moving a heavy piece of furniture
i. piloting and co-piloting an airplane
j. playing ping pong
k. doing a ballet number
l. playing hide and seek
m. acting the balcony scene from *Romeo and Juliet*
n. competing in a horse race
o. an M.D. and a nurse working on a patient in the operating room
p. presenting a comedy routine and being heckled
q. rooting for opposing sports teams
r. performing a synchronized swimming routine

s. setting up a tent for camping

t. decorating for the prom

10. For this exercise, divide into groups of four. One of you is the host of a party to which you've invited fairy tale characters. The trouble is you can't recognize them because it's a costume party. The guests have to act out their character so well that you can figure out who they are.

Each person should have a turn being the host, which means that each person also has to play three different roles.

11. Again, divide into groups of four. This time the party is being held for famous television characters, human or animal; flesh and blood or cartoon. The host has to guess who you are. This is a strange party in that the three characters attending the party don't know who the host is supposed to be. While the host is figuring out who you are, you have to figure out who he or she is.

Each of the following exercises has several parts to it. In the first two parts, you get into various positions and then one of you delivers a line suggested by the position. The line should be confrontational, that is, it should be something that demands an answer from the other character. This, in turn, produces conflict which you should try to build to a logical conclusion. After assuming the position and delivering the first line, you can change positions or move from place to place in whatever way you want.

Since you will be lying on the floor for some of the exercises, it might be a good idea to wear old clothes to class.

Working with a partner, build a scene from Part A and then Part B in whichever of the following exercises you choose. Each of the exercises should take no more than a minute.

111

Part 1

1A) Character 1: Stand, arms at your sides, staring at Character 2.
Character 2: Bend over with your knuckles touching the floor.
Line: Character 1 says, "You look like an ape!"

1B) Character 1: The only thing you should change about your previous position is that you should be in the middle of a shrug.
Character 2: Remain bent over as you were, but with your fingers instead of your knuckles touching the ground.
Line: Character 2 says, "If you weren't so out of shape, you could touch your toes too!"

2A) Character 1: Lie on your side with your head propped on one hand; you are very tired.
Character 2: Sit on the floor facing Character 1, your arms wrapped around your knees, also looking tired.
Line: Character 1 says, "We'll never find our way back, and it's all your fault."

2B) Character 1: Remain lying down but roll onto your stomach and lay your head on your arms.
Character 2: Remain sitting but point at Character 1.
Line: Character 2 says, "Can't you get anything right?"

3A) Character 1: Sit in a chair, hands in your lap.
Character 2: Stand behind Character 1 with one of your hands on Character 1's shoulders.
Line: Character 1 says, "Go ahead and try it; you don't scare me."

3B) Character 1: Lean forward in the chair and place your head in your hands.
Character 2: Stand in the same position but throw back your head and laugh.
Line: Character 2 says, "Did you really think you were going to get away with it?"

4A) Character 1: Stand on tiptoes and reach toward the ceiling.
Character 2: Stand facing Character 1 with your hands on your hips.
Line: Character 1 says, "This is the way you're supposed to do it."

4B) Character 1: Still on tiptoes, raise your arms so that they are straight out from the sides of your body.
Character 2: Keep the same position except that you should clasp your hands on top of your head.
Line: Character 2 says, "Sure, the tight rope's easy to walk when it's six inches off the ground. Just wait till you're twenty feet high."

5A) Character 1: Sit in a chair with one hand covering your mouth, the other resting in your lap.
Character 2: Stand with one hand against the side of your face, the other at your side.
Line: Character 1 says, "I can't believe you said that."

5B) Character 1: Sit with both hands in your lap.
Character 2: Both hands should be at your side, fists clenched.
Line: Character 2 says, "You may think it's funny, but I'm insulted."

6A) Character 1: You are bent over obviously picking something up.
Character 2: Stand facing Character 1 but look at the ground.
Line: Character 1 says, "Well, here it is. But don't you dare lose it again."

6B) Character 1: Stay in the same position, but this time clutch your right side with both hands.
Character 2: The only thing different is that you stare at Character 1 with a smug look on your face.
Line: Character 2 says, "Don't tell me a little thing like that hurts."

Part 2

For the second section of the five exercises, assume the same positions as before but begin with the following lines.

1A) Character 1 says, "That's the poorest excuse for weight lifting I've ever seen."
1B) Character 2 says, "You going to help me lift this rock or aren't you?"

2A) Character 1 says, "If you think I'm going to help with your bed, you're crazy. I already put up the tent."
2B) Character 2 says, "Get up right now, and do your chores."

3A) Character 1 says, "That's supposed to be a massage?"
3B) Character 2 says, "You can fool your father (or your mother) with that 'sick' routine, but you can't fool me."

4A) Character 1 says, "Don't ever throw your ball up on the roof again."
4B) Character 2 says, "Aren't you a little old to be playing 'airplane?'"

5A) Character 1 says, "Bad breath! You tell me I have bad breath!"
5B) Character 2 says, "You want to know the right way to push the wheelbarrow?"

6A) Character 1 says, "You want to know how to pull up the crab grass? This is the way to pull up the crab grass."
6B) Character 2 says, "I told you that isn't the side your appendix is on."

Part 3

Assume the same positions but come up with your own opening
   lines. Make the line confrontational or challenging.

Each person in class should have a turn at each of the parts.

   For the next exercise, again work with a partner. Let the person
show you a physical position to assume. Then you figure out one
for your partner. One of you should come up with an opening line
that fits the positions and which is confrontational or challenging.
Present a thirty-second to one-minute scene using the line.
   Once more assume the same position, and the other person
should come up with an opening line that leads to an improvisation.

   This exercise, just the opposite of the last, has several parts.

Part 1

   Work with the same partner or choose a different one. Decide
on an opening line from the following list. Now assume positions
that point up that line. For instance, in Number 6 one partner may
be bent over as if cleaning something from the floor. The other
could be standing with hands on hips.
   One of you should deliver the line, which is meant to evoke a
response. The other partner then should answer you. Keep on
exchanging dialog to build a thirty-second to one-minute scene.

   1. What's so good about that?
   2. You're not going to scare anyone that way.
   3. I think you'd better start over.
   4. Yeah, well I just don't think it's fair.
   5. Who told you to do it that way?
   6. What a mess!
   7. I'm sorry, but I couldn't help it.
   8. Can't you give me some help here?

9. If you'd watch where you're going, this sort of thing wouldn't happen.
10. I can't believe you broke it. I really can't.
11. Who let you in here anyhow?
12. Here, let me show you the right way to dribble the ball.
13. Be careful with that drill.
14. You're going to kill yourself if you keep that up.
15. Don't be such an idiot.

Part 2

With a partner make your own list of lines; trade papers with someone else and do an improv based on one or two of the lines you've received.

Part 3

Have someone in class place you in a particular physical position. Based on the position, do a thirty-second monolog that leads to a logical conclusion.

Chapter Nine
Character and Object Improvs

If you've never played charades, now is your chance. However, you're going to play a little bit differently than usual.

1. You are going to play as if you were such things as:

a. a historical figure
b. an animal
c. a TV or film star

Spend one third of the class time you devote to charades to each of these. It probably will work best to have four or five people on a team, which means you may want to spend two or three days on charades to give everyone a chance to participate. If you don't know how to play, allow your teacher or someone else in the classroom to explain. It's easy once you learn a few of the signals. After that, it's simply acting things out to convey a book title, a film, a TV show, a song title, etc., to the other players on your side. Now, however, you must do this as someone or something other than yourself.

For example, if you choose someone from history, you have to figure out something characteristic of that person, something that you can convey along with the subject of the charade. So not only must your side guess the title you've been given, but they also have to guess the person you're portraying. For instance, if you choose Napoleon Bonaparte, you may want to put the fingers of your hand inside the buttons of your shirt or top since most people are familiar with a painting of Napoleon in which he posed this way.

Or if you choose an animal — real or imaginary — determine one or more characteristics of the animal. For instance, if you choose a mouse, you might keep wiggling your nose.

For the TV or film star, you can choose to show a personal trait or one associated with a role.

Everyone should have at least three chances to present a title so you can appear as the historical figure, the animal, and the actor.

2. Again you are going to pretend to be someone other than yourself. Choose a celebrity such as a movie star or a sports figure. Then choose one of the following topics, all of which are nonsensical. You will have thirty seconds to prepare a one-minute monolog on the topic while at the same time you are portraying a celebrity. Have the rest of the class try to figure out whom you've chosen to play.

Don't worry about making sense with the monolog because you couldn't possibly do so. Do try to stick to the subject as silly it may be. Here are the topics:

a. How to Win Friends and Influence Domestic Animals
b. Study Tips for the Uninspired Student
c. Why a Groundhog Was Chosen to Predict the Weather
d. How to Choose the Right Equipment for Being Marooned on a Desert Isle
e. The High Cost of Snow Removal from the Martian Landscape
f. Why I'd Rather Be Human Than Ursine
g. The Time I Explored the Rings of Saturn
h. If I Were Emperor of the Moon
i. The Miracle Cream for a New and Better You
j. Snow Skiing in the Sahara
k. Being an Air-atarian; What's So Good About Eating Food
l. Two Steps to a Successful Career in Films
m. Learn Quantum Physics in Only Two Minutes a Day
n. How to Flunk Math and Graduate with Honors
o. Who Needs English Nohow

If you don't like any of these topics, come up with your own.

The only requirement is that they make little or no sense.

3. Choose a partner and pick out one of the following sets of traits. If you choose letter B, for instance, one of you then should decide to be *gossipy,* the other *snobbish.* Then choose an opening line from those listed below the traits. The idea is to present a scene in which you continuously display the trait you've chosen by what you say. This also should be a confrontational scene that builds to a high point.

For example, if you choose the line: "Why do you have to be that way?" either of you can start and immediately get into a disagreement.

Of course, if you choose *hateful* and *shy,* the person who is hateful probably is going to have to goad the shy person into answering.

Here are the traits:

    a. fickle/nagger
    b. gossipy/snobbish
    c. truthful/lazy
    d. hateful/shy
    e. boisterous/deceitful
    f. gluttonous/compassionate
    g. miserly/talkative
    h. disinterested/nosey
    i. boastful/reserved
    j. grumpy/loving
    k. egotistical/sincere
    l. selfless/ambitious
   m. worrier/confident
    n. greedy/fearful
    o. selfish/generous

Here are the lines:

    a. Why do you have to be that way?
    b. I'll be glad to get away from you.

c. Nobody could be as perfect as you think you are!

d. What are you trying to prove?

e. You don't know how to do anything right, do you?

f. You're such a phony.

g. Don't be such a goody-goody.

h. I'm sorry we ever met.

i. What's in it for me?

j. Who do you think you're fooling?

k. When I tell people what you're like, nobody's going to believe me.

l. It's all an act, isn't it?

m. I don't like your kind.

n. You've got to be kidding me!

o. How did I get stuck with you!

Come up with your own set of traits and your own opening lines for the exercise.

4. Again work with a partner and choose a trait from the following list. One of you starts the improv by saying to the other: "Why are you so _____?" and filling in the blank with a trait from the list. With the opening line as the beginning, do a one-minute improv.

a. lazy

b. ignorant

c. weird

d. silly

e. piggish

f. idiotic

5. Choose a partner; one of you is highly emotional, the other has ice water in her veins. One becomes upset at even the smallest things; not even an earthquake would bother the other.

Have a confrontation between the two of you using the lines that follow, none of which deals with earth-shattering events. Pretend that neither of you can understand the other's feelings or lack of them. Feel free to exaggerate as much as you like.

a. Did you hear that the game has to be canceled due to flooding?
b. Did you hear that Jerry broke his big toe?
c. Did you hear that school is going to be dismissed early tomorrow?
d. Did you hear that some girl fell down in gym and bruised her knee?
e. Did Jill tell you she isn't going to graduate?
f. Did you hear that we won the tournament championship?
g. Did you hear that Art forgot his lines opening night of the play?
h. Did you hear that we're supposed to have the first snowfall tomorrow?
i. Did you hear that Mrs. Johnson is going to retire?
j. Did you hear that Tom is moving out of state?

After you've gone through the exercise once, switch roles so that the partner who was emotional now becomes the one who feels little emotion and vice versa.

6. In this exercise, you are to take any two of the following nouns and adjectives and tie them together in a logical way in a one- to two minute monolog. It is not necessary to begin with one of the words, although you should use the first one fairly close to the beginning. Nor is it necessary to end the monolog with the other word. However, you should lead up to it as the high point of your story. For instance, suppose you chose the words "teacher" and "ignorant." You might say something like this:

> I always felt stupid; I don't know why. Maybe because both my parents went to college, and I felt I couldn't begin to compete with them. And then there was my older brother George who won a full academic scholarship to State.
> So anyhow, I heard we were going to have this new *teacher* for math, and I always hated math.

That goes back to having my uncle as my seventh-grade teacher. He wanted to prove to everyone that he wasn't playing favorites, so he was really hard on me. Anyhow, I just got by with Bs and Cs in every math class I took. So I dreaded going to class, especially with a new teacher. I felt so dumb.

It was plane geometry and she asked me to come up to the board and prove one of the theorems ... or whatever. I always felt stupid when this kind of thing happened. Every time I went to the board, I froze up.

Anyhow, I'm standing there and she asks if I'm having trouble, and I say, "Yeah, I am." And I hear giggles from other people in the class. But then Mrs. Farnsworth — the new teacher — she says to me, "You're a good student. I can see by your record."

Me, a good student. No way, I want to say.

But she says, "I was looking through the records, and I'm glad I have you in class."

"Me!" I say.

She chuckled. "You don't believe me?"

"I believe you," I said. But I was thinking how dumb I feel, how *ignorant*. She says to me, "It's okay if you don't know what to say. After all, you're here to learn, and you should never be ashamed of not knowing the answer." She turned to the class and said something like, "You know, there's a big difference between not knowing something — being ignorant, if you will — and not being able to learn. Ignorance is fine. It just shows that you don't have knowledge that maybe you should have. It doesn't mean you aren't able to learn it."

She sent me back to the seat and showed me what I should have done. And you know, ever after that I realized I wasn't so dumb. And it was just fine to be ignorant.

Here is the list of words for Exercise 6. Choose any two you like:

car	house	tree
fence	skunk	desk
rotten	ugly	gorgeous
lovely	stinking	computer
teacher	uncle	governor
estate	asylum	physical
emotion	alkey	fingers
clock	pencil	tissue
tooth	claws	bed
red	cozy	fireplace
oven	table	chair
ignorant	ill-advised	haircut
paper	scissors	rat
uninformed	apple cart	crate
engine	strawberries	stake
zombie	rapid-fire	black
singer	iceberg	bluish
young	hard	angel
kind	thoughtful	snug
tacky	snoopy	colorful
hazy	flavorful	goose
glorious	cheap	expensive
economical	horse	girl
rattlesnake	hen	dove

7. This exercise is similar to Exercise 6, except that you are to draw two sentences together logically. You need to choose a partner and then agree on one of the sets of sentences. They are nonspecific so you can interpret and use them in any number of ways.

Here's a brief example of the sort of thing to do. This is taken from letter "c" in the list.

CHARACTER 1: He's here already.
CHARACTER 2: Who is?

CHARACTER 1: Uncle Dan?
CHARACTER 2: I didn't know he was coming.
CHARACTER 1: Mom told us.
CHARACTER 2: He's weird.
CHARACTER 1: That's not nice to say.
CHARACTER 2: No, but it's true.
CHARACTER 1: Is it?
CHARACTER 2: Yeah?
CHARACTER 1: Why do you say that?
CHARACTER 2: He always dresses in black.
CHARACTER 1: So what?
CHARACTER 2: I hate black.
CHARACTER 1: Why do you hate it?
CHARACTER 2: It's depressing. It's like you're in mourning or something.
CHARACTER 1: He has to wear it, doesn't he?
CHARACTER 2: Well, I guess so ... since he's a priest.
CHARACTER 1: So he's not so weird after all, right?
CHARACTER 2: Maybe not, but you know something. Black is not my favorite color!

One of you should decide to use the first line, the other the second. You can take a few minutes to discuss how you are going to present a scene using the sentences.

Here is the list:

a. It's too hot.	The car stopped.
b. Where are you going?	Soon it will be time.
c. He's here already.	Black is not my favorite color.
d. Who's there?	The bat flew into the glass pane.
e. Well, look who made it.	Why is it always me?
f. They never showed up.	The gate sags.
g. That clock is fast.	Spring is my favorite time of year.
h. Did it wake you up too?	I read a story about that once.
i. Most of the audience left.	Time to mow the grass, I guess.
j. Do you like him?	She has a terrific voice.

k. I love your cat.	The paint really smeared.
l. I hate tossed salad.	My sister works in a hospital.
m. I'm out of here!	That's my favorite TV show.
n. The roof leaks.	I love to go to the beach.
o. It's a good book.	That picture's crooked.
p. The aerial blew down.	No way!
q. Why study calculus?	Her favorite color is purple.
r. What a song!	The sky is so blue today.
s. How about a pizza?	He's not been feeling well for a long time now.
t. He'd rather swim than do anything else.	Did you see today's paper?
u. He couldn't find his gray slacks.	Why are you serving the pie now?
v. That was the last time I saw her.	What's your favorite food?
w. That was some rain we had.	I've never used a typewriter.
x. But that was last summer.	I just got new tires.
y. You have smudges all over the paper.	I never liked jazz.
z. That color suits you.	It's one of the few birds that doesn't fly.
a-1. When I was a kid, I had this teddy bear	Wow, this apple is sour.
b-1. It's in the bookcase.	The museum is closed this morning.
c-1. The wastebasket's full.	It certainly is a nice day.
d-1. It's important to wear a hat in wintertime.	I wouldn't have the patience to be a farmer.

8. In this exercise, two people confront each other. The first says one of the following lines filling in the blank. Then the second tries to convince the first person that he or she is wrong. The improv should last about a minute.

    a. The problem with you is _____ .
    b. The problem with adults is _____ .
    c. The problem with teenagers is _____ .
    d. The problem with teachers is _____ .

9. Here's a similar exercise for two partners. Remember, however, that you are playing roles that you assume. The insults are not directed to you as a person. For the person giving the insults, stay away from anything that could be construed as personal. The purpose of the improv is to help you think fast and

to build confidence, not to tear anyone down.

One partner should deliver a line that starts dialog for a scene of thirty seconds to a minute. Then you should switch, and the other partner should deliver the line. This is what you say:

Here's what I think you should try to change about yourself: _____ .

10. Look at the following photos and choose one of them. From the way the person or sculpture is posed and the facial expressions, determine a logical mood. Then think of something you could say to the person or persons that would be appropriate. Tell them what you think they are feeling, how this makes you feel, and your response to them.

11. Choose a partner. Now choose two of the photos. Each of you should play one of the people in these photos. Decide on a topic you think would be logical for them to discuss. Using this topic, present a two-minute scene.

12. Choose another photo. In a monolog, talk to the person in the photo on whatever topic you think would be appropriate. Include an explanation of why you chose this particular person, why he or she appealed to you.

13. Choose still another photo. Pretending to be the person there, tell the rest of the class about your life or at least about an interesting incident in your life.

Chapter Ten

Opening Line Improvs

When you present improv in a theatre, the audience often is asked to supply lines or situations or various other ideas. The closest you can come to that in the classroom is to have those class members who are not participating in an improv at the time to serve as the "audience."

The first couple of exercises are to get you used to working with random lines.

1. Following are a list of orders for one actor to give another. Each should start a scene of conflict, After working with those that follow, try the same sort of thing with members of the class supplying lines. Once again, work in pairs and present a scene that begins with any of the following. Other than deciding who's going to give the opening line, do not do any planning for this improv.

    a. Get me a soda.
    b. Go outside and bring in the mail.
    c. Don't make so much noise.
    d. How can I hear the TV when you're banging away on the piano? I want you to stop it.
    e. Go fix me a sandwich.
    f. Clean up your room right now.
    g. I told you to finish your homework before you go out. Now do it.
    h. Go to your room
    i. Go get me a pen.
    j. Turn on the TV.
    k. Turn out the light.
    l. Get into this house right now.
    m. Pass me the potatoes.

n. Go upstairs and get my shoes.

o. Stop complaining.

For the second part of the exercise, choose a partner and go to the front of the room. The rest of the class should call out orders at random. Your teacher will decide which one you should use. Do not do any planning before you start.

2. This is similar to Exercise 1, though maybe a little bit more difficult. This involves working with random lines. Up until now, most of the improvs you've done have had conflict or at least some sort of interest built into them. Yet when you ask an audience for random lines, there's no knowing what sorts of answers you'll receive.

The lines that follow do not particularly inspire any sort of conflict or interest, so it's up to you to find some way of making them interesting. Choose one of the lines to begin a one- to two-minute monolog.

When everyone has finished the monolog, choose a partner. Now take a different line and use it as the basis of a scene. For instance:

CHARACTER 1: I just got a new pair of jeans.

CHARACTER 2: That's what you're wearing?

CHARACTER 1: Yes.

CHARACTER 2: I hope they didn't cost very much.

CHARACTER 1: What?

CHARACTER 2: I said I hope they didn't cost —

CHARACTER 1: I heard you.

CHARACTER 2: Then why did you ask?

CHARACTER 1: I couldn't believe you'd say that.

CHARACTER 2: I don't follow.

CHARACTER 1: You think my jeans are ugly or cheap or something.

CHARACTER 2: I never said anything like that.

CHARACTER 1: You didn't have to say it.

CHARACTER 2: Okay. I think your jeans ... are not very flattering.

CHARACTER 1: It's none of your business, really, is it?

CHARACTER 2: If you want to go around looking like a reject from a thrift store.

CHARACTER 1: Look who's talking.

CHARACTER 2: What do you mean!

After you've used these lines, the class can try to come up with others.

a. I lost my pen.

b. It rained a lot today.

c. I really hate Spanish class.

d. I go to the mall every weekend.

e. Did you see that new movie at the shopping center?

f. I hate turnips.

g. I wish school was out for the year.

h. I passed my driver's test.

i. I heard sirens blowing all night long.

j. I think every house on my street has a barking dog.

k. Did you see the basketball game on TV last night?

l. I can't go to the game this weekend.

m. I just got a new pair of jeans.

n. Mom lets me watch TV only one hour a night.

o. We went to that new Chinese restaurant last week.

p. Mom got way behind last week, so I had to help her with the laundry.

If you can get through lines such as these, it should be easy to field lines from the class or from an audience.

The rest of the class can now call out lines for each person. Your teacher will choose which of these you should use as the basis of a one- to two-minute monolog. Take no more than ten seconds or so to think what to say. Then begin delivering a monolog that begins with the line that was called out. Either provide conflict or

CHARACTER 1: Did you want me to wait on the corner all night?
CHARACTER 2: Would you do anything that dumb?
CHARACTER 1: So now you think I'm dumb?
CHARACTER 2: Did I say that?
CHARACTER 1: Do you think you have to say it outright for me to know what you mean?

5. Television shows and films often are about people in different occupations: lawyers, police officers, detectives, M.D.s, and so on. Build a short segment of a new television show around an occupation such as:

a. farming
b. welding
c. being a stenographer
d. teaching French
e. clerking at the cosmetics counter of a department store
f. gardening
g. being a meter maid
h. being a gas station attendant
i. being a plumber
j. being a cook
k. teaching aerobics
l. being an electrician
m. being a scene designer
n. being a newspaper boy or girl
o. being an office manager

Use one of these or any others that you can come up with. With one or two classmates, get together for two or three minutes and plan a scene that is suspenseful, exciting, and/or confrontational.

For example:

COSMETICS CLERK: *(Speaking as the Narrator)* He came into the store one day and demanded that new shade of lipstick, Baton Lip Rouge.

MAN: I want some lipstick, and I want it fast.

CLERK: What sort do you want, sir?

MAN: Whatever you got; I ain't picky.

CLERK: But, sir, I must know the shade.

MAN: Shade doesn't matter, I tell you.

CLERK: How about Baton Lip Rouge? It's all the rage.

MAN: Then give it to me; I ain't got all day.

CLERK: Are you sure, sir. It isn't for every woman, you know.

MAN: It's not for no woman at all.

CLERK: *(Shocked)* But, sir, I don't understand.

MAN: They're after me, see. I want to leave a message. I ain't got no paper. I ain't got no pen.

CLERK: Well, sir, our stationery department is right over there. You see, right near the side entrance.

MAN: Are you gonna give me the lipstick!

CLERK: All right, sir, here you are.

MAN: *(Plunking down twenty dollars)* Thanks, lady, just keep the change.

CLERK: *(As the narrator)* In all my years as a sales clerk, I never saw anything like it. He grabbed the lipstick without even waiting for a receipt. A few minutes later I heard gunfire, close like. I looked up and he was staggering through the stationery section, and out the side entrance. I guess he wanted a pen and paper after all. You know, I don't know what ever happened to that man. But I'll tell you something; he was no gentleman. I had my break coming up and I went into the ladies room. Right there on the mirror in the ladies' restroom in big scrawling letters, someone had written: "Tell Maggie I love her. The money's in the safety deposit box at First National." Here the letters got hard to read. It was something like, "I fooled them for the time being, Maggie. They'd never

133

try to make the monolog funny. Whatever you decide, the main objective is to keep the rest of the class interested.

3. Work in pairs. Get together to plan a scene of conflict, one that starts with a problem and builds to a climax. Now present the scene to the rest of the class. The catch is that in presenting it you can use only nonsense language.

You can, however, use movement, gestures, and facial expressions and you certainly can use tone of voice. The idea is that you should make the story so clear that your classmates have no difficulty in figuring out what it's about.

A variation of the exercise that you might try is to speak using only numbers.

4. This exercise is a little bit like Exercise 3, except here you have to give each response as a question which is a difficult thing to do. Work in pairs. One of you should decide on an opening question and then begin. When you can't think of anything else to say or fail to answer with a question, the scene is over. Try to see which pair of actors can go the longest.

Here's an example:

CHARACTER 1: What time are you leaving?
CHARACTER 2: When am I leaving?
CHARACTER 1: When are you leaving?
CHARACTER 2: Why do you want to know?
CHARACTER 1: Do you think I want to be left behind?
CHARACTER 2: Do you really think I'd leave you here?
CHARACTER 1: Oh, you've never left me before this?
CHARACTER 2: When did I ever leave you?
CHARACTER 1: Didn't we plan to go together to the game last weekend?
CHARACTER 2: Did you meet me on time?
CHARACTER 1: Didn't you show up at the wrong place?
CHARACTER 2: So what if I did?

look for me in here. But I know my time is short. Remember that I love you." It had to be that same man. No one else would do such a thing.

Never in all my life had I seen such a mess, and what a waste of an expensive lipstick. I wasn't going to have that sort of thing in my store! I took a paper towel and washed that mess right off the mirror. I hope I don't have to deal with this sort of thing again.

6. There are several types of improvisation you can do with objects. One is to have someone hand you an object at random and you tell a story about it, a story that is funny or otherwise interesting.

For this exercise, each of you can bring an object of some sort to school — an old toy or stuffed animal, a broken musical instrument, a tool such as a pipe wrench or a pair of pliers, a letter box or a lampshade. The important thing is that you have a variety of different pieces so that everyone can work with something different.

What happens is that you draw numbers or otherwise choose who goes first, second, and so on. The "moderator" (perhaps your teacher) will pick up one of the objects and hand it to you. You have fifteen seconds to think of something to tell the class about this object. You should then present a one- to two-minute monolog. For instance, suppose you receive an empty soda can:

> I was never allowed to drink sodas till I was eleven years old. Dad said the caffeine would stunt my growth. I tried to tell him that lots of sodas don't have caffeine, and anyhow he's six feet, nine inches tall, and he started drinking coffee when he was five years old. That's what grandma said. But dad won't listen.
>
> And Mom, you know what she says? She says if you get a nail and put it in a soda, the nail's going to disappear, the soda will eat it right up. She didn't

like it when I said if that was the case, maybe I better not drink any water either 'cause you know what happens to a nail in water, don't you?

Then for some reason, whatever it was, maybe Grandma talking some sense into my dad, or more than likely Mom getting tired of sneaking sodas she didn't think I saw her drinking, they let me try my first one.

Maybe I'm weird or whatever, but I had no idea what all the fuss was about. I didn't like it. It was a cola, a brand you're always hearing about. But I didn't like the way it stung my mouth and the way the bubbles went up my nose.

I told Mom that from then on I'd just drink water, rusty nails be darned. And if I really wanted a jolt of caffeine, I knew where she kept the coffee.

Anyhow, as a reminder of how bad the stuff was, I kept the can. Yes sir, this is it, my first can of soda. And my very last. And if you believe that, I guess you'll believe almost anything.

Instead of using a real object for this exercise, you can decide to use an object from one of the following photos and pretend it's the real thing. In fact, many times it works better not to use real props but imaginary ones. Once they are established, however, as the other elements of the scene, they cannot be changed in any way.

7. Get together with a partner and choose either a real object or one from the photo. Take a few minutes to plan how to use the object as the basis for a scene. For instance, suppose you chose a clay mask:

CHARACTER 1: That's my mask. Why do you have it?
CHARACTER 2: Your mask?
CHARACTER 1: It's been missing for several months. I always wondered what happened to it.

CHARACTER 2: You think I took your mask.

CHARACTER 1: Where did you get it?

CHARACTER 2: You do think I took it, don't you?

CHARACTER 1: I didn't say that. I just wonder where you got it.

CHARACTER 2: If you must know, my husband bought it for me. When he was in Africa.

CHARACTER 1: Your husband was never in Africa!

CHARACTER 2: Oh, so now I'm a liar as well as a thief.

CHARACTER 1: I mean I just didn't know your husband was ever in Africa.

CHARACTER 2: There are a lot of things you don't know about me.

CHARACTER 1: And a lot of things I do seem to know.

CHARACTER 2: What are you implying!

CHARACTER 1: I'm not implying anything. I'm saying it straight out. I'd like you to return my mask.

Of course, you can keep going from that point on till you reach a climax. It doesn't matter what object you choose. Almost anything can serve as the basis of a scene.

8. Five or six of you at a time should stand or sit in a straight line facing the rest of the class. Place to one side the objects everyone has brought to class. One of your classmates will pick up an object and hand it to the first person in line. This person will think of another object that is similar in some way. The idea then is to use the object as the thing you imagine it to be. When you finish, pass it on the next person in line. That person will pass it to the next one and so on. Each of you should try to come up with something different the object can be used for. For example, suppose the first thing that's chosen is a round rock.

The first person pretends it's a baseball and winds up ready to pitch it. The second person pretends it's a crystal ball, the third a lump of modeling clay, the fourth a ball to hang on a Christmas tree, the fifth an apple or a peach, and the sixth an egg. Pantomime using the object as whatever you pretend it is. For instance, the person who sees it as a crystal ball can hold his or her hands over it

pretending to be a fortune teller. The fourth person can pretend to hang it on a tree and then stand back and admire it. The idea is to make clear to the rest of the class or to an audience just what the object represents.

After everyone has a chance to use the same object, go to another one for as many times as you like.

9. Put yourself into the following photo so that in a scene you present you are inside the house.

Choose one thing from each of the following lists. Then take into consideration the type of house and what you think about when you see the picture. With two or three other partners play a three- to four-minute scene around the information you receive.

A: What happened in this house?
1. Someone was tied up in the basement.
2. Someone was murdered.
3. There was an international spy ring headquartered here.
4. The Mob used it as a secret hideout.

5. It was used to conduct unusual experiments.
6. It was used as a stop over for space travelers from other galaxies.
7. It was headquarters for a drug ring.
8. This is where the kidnapers stayed.
9. This is where they stored all the loot.
10. This is where they found all the runaways.

B. Someone said:
1. "It was the worse case of this kind they'd ever seen."
2. "The police were in on the whole thing."
3. "The body (or bodies) had been there a long time."
4. "They still haven't found the brains behind the operation."
5. "Those poor people never had a chance."
6. "Before this is over, it's going to affect the highest levels of government."
7. "It was a plot to take over the country."
8. "Nobody knows who owns the house."
9. "The neighbors didn't notice a thing."
10. "If it happened here, it can happen anywhere."

C. Here's where the house is located:
1. on a remote island.

2. right downtown in a major city.
3. in the richest suburb in town.
4. in the midst of a slum area.
5. right next to the offices of the city government.
6. behind a police station.
7. next to the busiest highway in the state.
8. in a gigantic space station the Russians have built.
9. in a gigantic underground cave.
10. in a sleepy little village.

D. Here's what I saw in one of the closets:
1. human skeletons.
2. several smelly dead bodies.
3. suitcases filled with money.
4. a major stash of food and water.
5. some poor kids all tied up and gagged.
6. a huge stash of illegal drugs.
7. more electronic equipment than I'd ever seen in my life.
8. several poor dogs that looked like they were starving.
9. enough clothes to outfit an army — men's, women's, children's.
10. roses; bunches and bunches of roses.
11. so many dishes you wouldn't believe.
12. books of every kind and description.
13. old CDs and tapes from the early 1990s.
14. broadcasting equipment.
15. boxes and boxes of remote controls.

Instead of choosing your own line, you might try the variation of writing each thing from each list on a separate slip of paper and then drawing a slip from each category so that you end up with a random choice. However you do it, use each of the elements in a scene that builds to a climax.

10. Something terrible happened on this beach, something so horrendous that local residents refuse to talk about it.

A reporter for a big city newspaper arrives in town with his photographer and tries to get to the bottom of the story. The reporter has a special interest in what happened because a younger sister lived here and hasn't been heard of since the very night it all happened. The reporter has little luck until one night he or she receives a note to come to the beach unarmed.

For this scene you need a reporter, a photographer, as many town residents as you want to use, and perhaps the younger sister. Using all the information and the photo itself, try to solve the mystery.

11. You and your best friends were walking down this country road when something happened that forever changed your world.

What was it? How did it happen? How did it affect you? In a three- to four-minute scene, show these things to the rest of the class. You need two or three friends and as many other characters as you think it will take.

12. Take a walk down this road. Who do you meet there? Think of something you would like to tell the person about your life? In a monolog of at least two minutes, tell them what it is. Now play the part of the person you meet and have that person tell you something.

13. Put yourself into this picture. Now tell your audience what life is like here — what you like about it, and what you don't like.

14. Choose a partner and take two or three minutes to plan a scene around one of the following paintings. Now present it to the class.

Chapter Eleven
Scene Improvs

So far you've been doing improvs only in class. There is a difference between what happens in class and what happens in a performance. In class, you're in a "safe" atmosphere where everyone accepts that you are learning. At times, you may even have stopped and started over, or your teacher may have stopped you and asked you to try something again. Of course, you cannot do that in performance.

Another difference is that a class is much more structured. Since the beginning, you've worked mostly with improv situations that were set up for you. It is possible to do this sort of thing in performance, but usually you rely on suggestions from the audience, and in most cases, an evening of improv deals largely with humorous scenes and monologs, though there can be serious moments as well.

Although the types of things included in a performance vary from group to group, generally you would present monologs and scenes, and work in one or more ways with objects, either real or imaginary.

Later in the chapter we'll work with what often is called "premises," which are ideas the audience calls out. When you ask the audience to give you ideas, you might be asked to present material about almost anything. That doesn't mean that you have to accept every idea. If you think the audience's suggestion is inappropriate, you can decline to use it and ask for another suggestion. But this should not often be the case.

In an earlier chapter you learned a number of rules about improv. Here are a few others:

1. As soon as possible, the actors in a scene need to establish:
    a. what the scene is about.
    b. who the characters are.
    c. where the action takes place.

2. You need to end a scene when appropriate. In one that has conflict, stop shortly after reaching the climax. If you're presenting another sort of scene, bring it to a definite conclusion. Every scene should have a definite beginning and a definite ending. Don't ramble and don't just stop abruptly. Don't ease into a scene or trail off at the end. If you are thinking throughout and following everything that happens, and if all the actors are supportive of each other, this should not be difficult.

3. You need to decide whether you are going to get together with the other actors before each scene to do any planning or whether you are simply going to start. It doesn't matter which you do except that if you do "huddle" beforehand, it should be for just a few seconds.

4. During each scene or monolog, take time to think. This somewhat contradicts the idea that you should say the first thing that comes into your mind. Certainly, you should be spontaneous in your responses, but then again you have to take into consideration everything that has been said and done in the scene. If it takes a second or two to recall anything important you need to remember, do take that time.

5. As you learned, all that is said or done in a scene or a monolog then becomes "fact." You then have to make sure that *all* of these facts play an important role in the improv. It would not come across well to have statements that then lead nowhere. For instance, if you're talking about a school dance and someone says, "Sally's mother wouldn't allow her to attend because her grandmother's arriving from out of town," you can't just drop this. There has to be reference later to Sally. Maybe she enters the scene

(the dance) late. Maybe everyone decides to go see her before going home after the dance. But once any element is introduced into a scene, you have to deal with it, or it will look as if it didn't belong.

6. The person who speaks first in a scene takes on a lot of responsibility for setting the action and giving an indication of what is to follow. Thus he or she needs to make sure that the action is pointed in the proper direction.

7. Use all of the stage. Don't confine yourself to just a small area. Early on, when you are just beginning to do improv, this might be difficult because you feel safer in a smaller area with smaller movements and gestures. But whether performing in the front of a classroom or on a stage in a theatre, use all the space that's available to you.

8. You can reveal your character in a number of ways without saying a word. Included are:

a. the way you walk and carry yourself.
b. the sorts of props you use.
c. your tone of voice.
d. the attitude you project.

Let's look more closely at these ways of revealing character. You can indicate age, mood and feelings, tiredness, and a lot of other things simply by the way you walk. You show that you are burdened down or lifted up, whether you're alert or simply uninterested.

Props can be very personal. Figure out what would be important or appropriate to your character and then use it. An imaginary prop can be just as effective and often more effective than a real one. Figure out how the character you've assumed would hold the prop. If it's close to the chest, this can show the object is important to the person. If it's held carelessly, this may indicate that the character is happy-go-lucky or fails to take responsibility.

Tone of voice conveys feelings and personality. A whiny voice tells the audience something different about a character than does a grating voice. Tone of voice also indicates emotions.

Your attitude is a combination of all these things, and once you've established it, once you've established the way your character views the world, you have to maintain this attitude. The character has to be consistent even when showing a variety of emotions.

Movement and Stance

1. In the following, indicate the character by the way you hold yourself, stand, and walk. The audience should be able to tell a lot about the type of person. With some of these, it shouldn't even be too difficult to guess exactly what you are portraying.

Don't take the easy way out. Don't run as the runner or dance as the dancer. Make the performance more subtle.

Before you start, determine what is typical about the person. How is he or she similar to others in the same category? Now do the opposite and determine differences. If you are portraying an old man, consider that each is different from any other. One may compete in the Senior Olympics while another has been inactive most of his life. One may have severe arthritis; another may have no severe ailments. One may be thin, another overweight.

Once you've worked with the following, come up with examples of your own.

    a. an eighty-five-year-old man
    b. a boy or girl in the primary grades
    c. a teenager who is very happy
    d. an old woman who is depressed
    e. a ballet dancer
    f. a wrestler
    g. a long-distance runner
    h. a mother who is grieving
    i. a shy teenager
    j. a bully

k. an important political figure
l. a middle-aged, male extrovert
m. a pious woman
n. a nerd
o. a self-assured, teenaged girl
p. a new mother
q. an insecure, middle-aged man
r. an actress in a highly successful television series
s. an Olympic swimmer
t. an operatic tenor

2. Choose a character you want to portray. It can be from the above list or something entirely different. Now choose a prop, real or imaginary, that will help you portray the character, one that can help show the person's attitudes, feelings, and outlook on life. You can move or sit or stand in whatever ways you wish. The only rule is that you cannot talk. See if the rest of the class can figure out what it is you want to show about the character.

3. Choose a character and a prop, again real or imaginary. Show the significance of the prop to the character. To do this, you should know in your own mind why the prop is important and what it signifies.

4. This exercise approaches the use of objects or props in a different way. Choose a partner, and agree on a prop to use in a scene. Now focus on it to show how important it is.

For instance, you might choose a basketball that you bounce once or twice before placing it in the center of the room. Throughout the scene, you keep glancing at the ball, occasionally picking it up and holding it before placing it back on the floor. Whatever actions you perform, make sure they direct the audience's attention to the basketball. Yet do not mention it in the dialog. For example:

FATHER: *(Bounces a basketball and then puts it down.)* I was thinking of that first game.

149

MOTHER: When Billy was in seventh grade.

FATHER: Seems like only yesterday.

MOTHER: It was years ago, Tom.

FATHER: He was a good kid. Why do these things always happen to the good kids?

MOTHER: Remember how he always used to help me? Carrying in groceries, moving the furniture so I could clean.

FATHER: Or simple things. Like that time I needed him to hold a flashlight so I could change a flat tire, and I couldn't get it changed! It was raining hard. He stood there all that time, rain pouring down his face and soaking his clothes. *(Picking up the ball, cradling it in his arm.)*

MOTHER: We'd better go, Tom.

FATHER: Coach Richards said the entire team's going to be there.

MOTHER: Except for ... *(She cries quietly.)*

FATHER: *(He places the ball once more in the middle of the floor and crosses to MOTHER. He puts an arm around her shoulder.)* It's not fair, Katy. It's not fair!

This scene has little conflict. Yet there is a definite beginning and a definite end, despite not knowing exactly what occurred. We can only guess that it was something terrible and that it involved the son and that apparently the parents are now headed to some sort of memorial service in his honor.

The scene is indicative of the type that is built around an idea rather than a plot. Everything in it contributes to the idea that something happened to the boy and the parents are grieving. It's made even more poignant by the fact that the ball is never mentioned but we know that it or the game of basketball was very important to the boy thus to his parents.

Building a scene from a prop is more the type of thing you might have to do in an evening of improvisation where ideas usually are not fleshed out, and there is at best very little given in

150

the way of background or characters or action.

With your partner, try to build a scene around one of the following props. It can be a serious scene such as the sample, or you can make it funny. Take a minute to decide on the prop and then how you are going to use it. You can refer to it in dialog or not. The only requirements are that the prop be the focus of the scene, and that the scene itself have a definite structure.

a. a pen
b. a hat or cap
c. a small clock
d. a bracelet
e. a jacket
f. a telephone
g. a painting or photo
h. a tape dispenser
i. a paint brush
j. a ceramic figurine
k. a stuffed animal
l. a baseball glove
m. a wagon
n. a book
o. a remote control for a TV set
p. a sweater
q. a greeting card
r. a letter
s. a baton
t. a tennis racquet

5. Although an evening of improv can take any number of directions, you may want to include some monologs. You can ask the audience for a premise ... a theme or subject, an object, or a color. Then you need to come up with something specific that is based on this, and you have to come up with a structure.

Suppose, for instance, that someone suggested the color red:

I remember my mother's red dress, the dress my father gave her for Christmas one year when I was in junior high. It was beautiful, the kind that almost floats by itself when you move. I loved that dress. My mother loved it too. She wore it everywhere, to the family gatherings we had that Christmas at each of our Grandma and Grandpa's houses. To the concert at school. It was like she didn't ever want to wear another.

Then she wore it to church, and all the old ladies and all the old men were scandalized.

"Why, in my day," they said, "no one would dare wear something like that to church."

"It cheapens things, that's what it does."

"What sort of woman would it take to wear such a thing?"

I remember Mom's overhearing what these people said, and I knew it hurt her. It spite of it all, she held her head up high. On the way home in the car, I could see tears in her eyes. She went up to her room and took off the dress and hung it in her closet. She came down wearing an old dress, pale blue, made of wool.

I never saw her wear the red dress again. Soon it disappeared from the closet. But I remember it and how much I loved it and how beautiful it was. I wonder if Mama remembers it too.

It can help if you have a grain of truth in what you say. Maybe your mother did have a red dress that you particularly liked. Maybe people somewhere did say bad things you overhead about what someone was wearing. When you base a monolog on what really happened, you don't have to stick to the truth throughout. You can change and add to fit whatever you want to say.

Take one of the following and develop it into a monolog.

a. green
b. comet
c. dog
d. family car
e. school desk
f. rainy day
g. streetlight
h. driveway
i. farmhouse
j. skyscraper
k. jaywalker
l. sand
m. vase
n. lawn chair
o. patio
p. cotton
q. surf
r. lilies
s. tomato
t. clothes basket
u. dresser
v. microwave oven
w. good luck charm
x. name tag
y. paperweight

Now present a monolog based on a word in the list or on words suggested by someone else in the class.

6. Work in groups of five or six and decide which of you is going to start. The first person should say the opening sentence of an original story that the group will create. As soon as he or she finishes, the next person in line should say a second sentence, the next person a third one and so on until everyone has given just one sentence. Then go back to the first person and continue on until the story is complete.

This exercise illustrates how well you have to listen to what is going on so that when it's your turn, you can continue without hesitation. Don't pause; don't wait till a better idea occurs to you. Don't try to think ahead to where you want the story to go because as soon as you do, you lose track of what is happening. And by the time it's your turn, the piece may have taken an entirely different direction from the one you planned.

Often an improv group will present the entire evening's entertainment around one theme. Or something in the opening will suggest a related topic. For example, the red dress monolog may inspire a piece about Christmas or about going to church or about an important article of clothing.

In the next exercise, as usual, you need to keep in mind everything that has been said and done. Of course, you can introduce new material, so long as it is consistent with what has preceded it. And you can change the direction of the story, with the same restriction.

This can be something like the monolog about the red dress, which was built around a theme, or it can be a story with a plot. It doesn't matter.

7. This is similar to something you've done in earlier chapters where you based a scene on an opening line of dialog. Here, however, you take your opening line from a play and build a scene on it. Shakespeare works well for this sort of thing. For example, you could begin with "Murder most foul," which is from *Hamlet*.

CHARACTER 1: Murder most foul.
CHARACTER 2: Who murders fowl?
CHARACTER 1: I didn't say anyone murdered fowl.
CHARACTER 2: I heard you say it myself.
CHARACTER 1: "Murder most foul," I said.
CHARACTER 2: See! You're telling me to kill chickens, and ducks, and geese, and —

CHARACTER 1: Enough!

CHARACTER 2: You've changed your mind? Now that I've listed the things you want dead.

CHARACTER 1: I don't want them dead.

CHARACTER 2: And a good thing too that you changed your mind.

Well, you could go on and on with such as scene, which obviously is just for fun. With a partner or partners, choose one of these opening lines and present a scene around it.

a. That he is mad, 'tis true. *(Hamlet)*

b. What bloody man is that? *(Macbeth)*

c. Hang out our banners on the outward walls. *(Macbeth)*

d. I am not bound to please thee with my answer. *(Merchant of Venice)*

e. He wears the rose of youth upon him. *(Antony and Cleopatra)*

f. Sweep on, you fat and greasy citizens. *(As You Like It)*

g. I do not like her name. *(As You Like It)*

h. Cupid is a knavish lad ... *(Midsummer Night's Dream)*

i. Keep up your bright swords, for the dew will rust them. *(Othello)*

j. O! Thereby hangs a tale. *(Othello)*

k. You told a lie, an odious damned lie ... *(Othello)*

l. A plague o' both your houses! *(Romeo and Juliet)*

m. Tempt not a desperate man. *(Romeo and Juliet)*

n. Kiss me Kate, we will be married o' Sunday. *(Taming of the Shrew)*

o. Your tale, sir, would cure deafness. *(Taming of the Shrew)*

p. If music be the food of love, play on ... *(Twelfth Night)*

q. He's as tall a man as any in Illyria. *(Twelfth Night)*

r. Nothing emboldens sin so much as mercy. *(Timon of Athens)*

s. Who is Sylvia? *(Two Gentlemen of Verona)*

t. I am a feather for each wind that blows. *(The Winter's Tale)*

You might try the same sort of thing taking lines from well known poems or any other form of literature.

8. You can do this exercise from any starting point — a line in a play, a color, a noun, or opening lines of dialog. There are four characters. Two act out a story on stage, but they don't speak. Two others stand on either side of the playing area pretending to be the voices of the other two. The two who are doing the pantomime try to tell a story by their actions. The two who act as the voices must try to follow the story and use appropriate dialog to accompany the pantomime, dialog that is logical and furthers the story.

Four of you should get together and decide which of you will perform pantomime and which will do the voices. Once you've completed a two- to three-minute scene, switch places so that those who spoke now present a pantomime, and those that presented the pantomime now become the voices.

Here are a combination of things to choose from in presenting a scene. Use whichever of these appeals to you.

a. opening dialog:
1. "I hate to go downtown anymore."
   "What kind of an attitude is that?"
2. "It must be getting pretty late."
   "Please don't leave. I don't want to be alone."
3. "I left the money right here."
   "You mean someone took it!"
4. "Did you hear what happened to Ben?"
   "Yeah, I heard all right."
5. "Have you made up your mind if you're going?"
   "I don't have much choice, do I?"

b. random words
1. coffin
2. fireplace
3. cold
4. pigs
5. cider
6. roasting
7. meowing

8. trailer
9. bluegrass
10. wig

c. objects
1. a brick
2. a crayon
3. a purse
4. earphones
5. a cardboard box
6. an answering machine
7. a bicycle
8. a pipe wrench
9. a video camera
10. a CD

9. For this exercise, think of a fairy tale. Get together with as many other classmates as you need to fill the roles and show what happened after the fairy tale ends. For instance, show what happened to Chicken Little and all those characters who were hit in the head when the sky was falling. Maybe they've all had concussions and had to be treated at a local hospital. Maybe the falling objects caused amnesia or brain damage.

10. Choose a partner, and then each of you pick a well-known saying from the following list. At the same time, each of you should act out this adage in front of the class. For instance, if you choose, "It is more blessed to give than to receive," you can keep trying to give things to your partner — presents, money, food, sodas, or whatever else you can think of. At the same time, be very adamant in your refusal to take anything whatsoever from anyone else. While you are doing this your partner can be trying to keep a bird from flying out of his or her hand and pointing to other birds to illustrate that "A bird in the hand is worth two in the bush." See how long it takes the class to figure out what you are doing.

a. Early to bed, early to rise, makes a man healthy, wealthy, and wise.
b. An apple a day keeps the doctor away.
c. One good turn deserves another.
d. Too many cooks spoil the broth.
e. A fool and his gold are soon parted.
f. What goes up must come down.
g. A stitch in time saves nine.
h. A bird in the hand is worth two in the bush.
i. All's fair in love and war.
j. Once bitten, twice shy.
k. If you want something done, do it yourself.
l. All that glitters is not gold.
m. A penny saved is a penny earned.
n. Haste makes waste.
o. Don't look a gift horse in the mouth.
p. Don't count your chickens before they hatch.
q. You can't make a silk purse from a sow's ear.
r. It's not over till the fat lady sings.
s. People who live in glass houses shouldn't throw stones.
t. Beauty is only skin deep.
u. Fools rush in where angels fear to tread.
v. Good things come in small packages.
w. The early bird catches the worm.
x. Let sleeping dogs lie.
y. Beggars can't be choosers.
z. Don't put the cart before the horse.

Part Four

Improvising Plays

Chapter Twelve

Improvising Existing
Plays to Develop Characters

Directors often use improv to help the actors better grasp and understand existing plays. If actors are concerned about lines, the director may tell them to put away the book and go through a scene or an act paraphrasing what the playwright wrote. This helps build confidence since the actors usually see that they understand their characters, that they grasp the meaning of the play, and they can follow the play's progression.

Read through one of the following scenes a few times but make no attempt to memorize the words. Then choose a partner and without looking at the book, play through the scene using your own words.

The first is from a play titled *Choosers Can't Be Losers*.

Cast of Characters
WILL, 17
TIM, 14

SETTING: The action takes place on the back porch of a house in a small town. It's mid-October with just a hint of coming winter in the air.

AT RISE: WILL and TIM are sitting on the back porch steps.

WILL: Remember how we used to play pitch and catch with dad every Sunday afternoon?
TIM: Before we went to visit grandma.

WILL: We'd come home from church and Mom would be in the house fixing Sunday dinner ... which was really lunch.

TIM: Roast beef or chicken. And always that salad with a banana covered in peanut butter and mayonnaise sitting there on a leaf of lettuce. Remember?

WILL: Yeah. We had some good times then. Picnics, going to the park, camping each summer.

TIM: Not anymore, huh?

WILL: Maybe it's not so bad.

TIM: Guess you can say that.

WILL: I didn't mean —

TIM: You're the one who's staying here! I'm the one who has to — I hate it. I love Mom, but I love Dad too. And I don't want to leave. I want to stay where my friends are. Everyone I know lives here. Grandma and Grandpa.

WILL: Summer. School vacations. You'll come back then.

TIM: Once I'm gone ... I'll be a stranger.

WILL: You won't. You know what? You'll never be a stranger to me.

TIM: But you know how it is when kids move. They come back to visit, and it's like we never knew each other. Like they're the same person, and yet they're not. *(Beat)* Why are you the one who gets to stay!

WILL: We've been through this, Tim. It's my senior year. I can't leave right in the middle of it.

TIM: And the judge says one of us has to go, and that one has to be me.

WILL: You know she didn't say that.

TIM: But I had to choose! Didn't I? And I know how much you want to stay. I'm not really sorry I said I'd be the one. You know that, Will. But I wish —

WILL: If you're mad at me, I can understand.

TIM: Yeah, I guess I am mad ... but not at you. I'm going to some place where I don't know anybody, and things are different, and I can't come back except at certain times.

WILL: I'm going to miss Mom.

TIM: You trying to say I'm lucky that I'm going.

162

WILL: No ... But I'm sure you'll miss Dad?

TIM: I'll miss him. Like we were just saying. Playing pitch and catch. *(Beat)* Why can't they work it out!

WILL: They can't; that's all there is to know.

TIM: Why not, damn it! It's not fair to do this to me. To both of us.

WILL: Maybe it isn't fair to want them to stay together.

TIM: I'm going to miss you, Will. *(Tears in his eyes; trying to keep his voice from breaking)* I guess you're not supposed to say that kind of stuff to a big brother. Not supposed to cry either.

WILL: It's okay.

TIM: Are you going to miss me, Will?

WILL: I'll miss you. *(Punches TIM lightly on the shoulder.)* Look, little bro, we have to get going. Mom will be picking you up in just a few minutes.

TIM: Pitch and catch with Dad. We always used to play pitch and catch. You know something, Will?

WILL: Yeah?

TIM: I guess we're too old to play pitch and catch anymore.
(The lights fade to black.)

Following is a short play called *The Other Side of the Fence.* You can try paraphrasing the entire play or just one of the scenes.

Cast of Characters:
CASSIE, 15-17
DENISE, 15-17.

SCENE 1

SETTING: The action occurs in the bedrooms of CASSIE and DENISE, connected only by telephone. Beside CASSIE is a large pile of cotton-balls or bunting.

AT RISE: CASSIE is sitting in a chair beside her desk. DENISE is sitting on a chair by a small table.

NOTE: The girls are normal in appearance except that they wear large bags or sacks around their necks. Cassie's is empty; Denise's is filled to overflowing with cotton. Throughout the first scene DENISE keeps taking cotton out of her sack and placing it on the floor by her desk. CASSIE, on the other hand, keeps picking up cotton and stuffing it into her bag. By the end of the scene, all the cotton on the floor by Cassie's desk is in her bag; all the cotton that was in Denise's bag is now on the floor.

CASSIE: I've always envied you, Denise.

DENISE: Envied me?

CASSIE: Your figure's so perfect. I've always wanted a figure like yours.

DENISE: You've got to be kidding. I'm ... Okay, Cassie, I wouldn't admit this to anyone else. I'm fat. God knows, I'm fat.

CASSIE: What?

DENISE: You said you envy me. Well, I've always envied you.

CASSIE: Me? What for?

DENISE: Your figure!

CASSIE: Mine! That doesn't make sense.

DENISE: Pencil-thin. That's what I've always wanted to be.

CASSIE: I'm nothing but a sack of bones.

DENISE: You're not!

CASSIE: And you're not fat!

DENISE: I'll tell you something.

CASSIE: What?

DENISE: I've been dieting.

CASSIE: Dieting. But I told you ... You look great.

DENISE: DON'T LIE TO ME! *(Beat)* I'm sorry. I didn't meant to yell.

CASSIE: I wasn't lying. I think your figure's fantastic. I wish I looked like you.

DENISE: Stop it, will you!

CASSIE: What!

DENISE: Lying!

CASSIE: I told you!

DENISE: All right. Just don't ... flatter me then.

CASSIE: Flatter! You won't believe me, will you?

DENISE: Believe what you said? No way. *(Chuckles.)* If we lived hundreds of years ago ... maybe then I'd believe you.

CASSIE: A hundred years!

DENISE: In art class, we're studying old painters — like Rubens. Anyhow, they liked their women fat. Round. Plump. Their models. Haven't you seen pictures of the paintings?

CASSIE: My God, Denise, you don't think you look like that!

DENISE: Like overstuffed sausage or Humpty Dumpty or a big fat balloon.

CASSIE: You're not like those pictures.

DENISE: What pictures?

CASSIE: The paintings! You don't look like that. You're just the right weight. Just what you should be.

DENISE: Oh, sure, if I want to get a job in a circus. Ladies and gentlemen, step right up. It quivers, it jiggles. It's a living, breathing blob. The one and only Denise, the world's obesest woman.

CASSIE: *(Laughs.)* Obesest?

DENISE: Okay, maybe I got a little carried away. But like I said, I'm on a diet.

CASSIE: What kind?

DENISE: It's fantastic. For a week you drink nothing but water.

CASSIE: Water.

DENISE: Yes.

CASSIE: But what do you eat?

DENISE: Eat? All you do is drink. And the pounds melt away.

CASSIE: That could be dangerous. Besides, it's silly. You don't need to do that.

DENISE: Says you.

CASSIE: Please, Denise, don't do anything silly.

DENISE: What's silly about losing weight?

CASSIE: Nothing, I guess. If you're fat.

DENISE: I'm fat! Obese! Grossly overweight! Two-ton Tillie!

CASSIE: Stop it. *(Beat)* I mean it, Denise. This could be dangerous.

DENISE: People fast all the time.

CASSIE: And some of them die.

DENISE: You're as bad as my mom.

CASSIE: It can be a shock to the system.

DENISE: I'll tell you what's a shock.

CASSIE: What!

DENISE: Looking in the mirror and seeing all that fat.

CASSIE: Yeah, well, I wish I could see what you see.

DENISE: What!

CASSIE: I mean it. *(Beat)* You said you're on a diet.

DENISE: Yeah?

CASSIE: Me too.

DENISE: You, on a diet. But you look perfect, why would you go on a diet?

CASSIE: I told you.

DENISE: You told me that you wished — who knows why? — that you were fat like me.

CASSIE: I said I want a figure like yours.

DENISE: You wish you were fat!

CASSIE: No, no, no! Don't you know how good you look?

DENISE: Okay, okay. I'll accept that you think I look good.

CASSIE: I do think so.

DENISE: That's what I said.

CASSIE: You just don't understand, do you?

DENISE: What?

CASSIE: How good you look.

DENISE: Oh, yeah?

CASSIE: Yeah!

DENISE: If I look so darned good — Okay, yeah, if fat is so great, then why are you — of all the people I know — on a diet.

CASSIE: What!

DENISE: A diet. Why are you on a diet? If there's one person in the whole world who doesn't need to lose weight, it's you.

CASSIE: Lose weight.

DENISE: That's what I said.

CASSIE: I don't want to lose weight.

DENISE: You said you were on a diet.

CASSIE: I am on a diet.

DENISE: I rest my case.

CASSIE: You think all diets are to help *lose* weight.

DENISE: They aren't?

CASSIE: No! I found this article for people like me. About people like me.

DENISE: People like you?

CASSIE: People so thin you can't see them if you look at them sideways.

DENISE: I can't believe you feel like that.

CASSIE: Like what!

DENISE: That you're too skinny or something.

CASSIE: I'm way too skinny.

DENISE: You're not.

CASSIE: Uh huh, and Brad Pitt's never starred in a movie. And Washington, DC isn't the nation's capitol, and the planet we live on is not named —

DENISE: All right, I get your point! Not that I understand it. I mean, I understand what you're saying. But it doesn't make sense.

CASSIE: Well, it doesn't make sense that you think you're fat.

DENISE: Right, I'm not fat. Like an elephant's not fat. Like trees don't grow leaves. Like we don't need oxygen to breathe. Like —

CASSIE: Don't get carried away. I get your point too. But I don't understand it either.

DENISE: Maybe if you had to carry around all this excess poundage.

CASSIE: Excess!

DENISE: What I started to say before I was so rudely interrupted —

CASSIE: Interrupted!

DENISE: See what I mean?

CASSIE: Do you want to hear about my diet or not?

DENISE: So tell me.

CASSIE: It's to gain weight. It's not necessarily how much you eat, but what you eat.

DENISE: What do you mean?

CASSIE: Really rich food. Gravy and ice cream and thick chocolate syrup.

DENISE: Stop it, for God's sake, stop it.

CASSIE: What's the matter?

DENISE: You're making me ill.

CASSIE: You don't like ice cream and chocolate syrup!

DENISE: Just thinking about them makes me — ooh!

CASSIE: Makes you what?

DENISE: Nothing.

CASSIE: Makes you what!

DENISE: All right! Makes me gag. Makes me puke. Makes me vomit, throw up, regurgitate —

CASSIE: Why are you doing this?

DENISE: What? You asked me, and I told you.

CASSIE: And you didn't exaggerate just the tiniest bit.

DENISE: I didn't.

CASSIE: Nevertheless, it's what I'm doing.

DENISE: What does your Mom say about all this?

CASSIE: She ...

DENISE: Come on. What does your mom think?

CASSIE: Maybe ... well, maybe she doesn't know —

DENISE: Doesn't know?

CASSIE: Okay, I fix things.

DENISE: Fix things?

CASSIE: Before she gets home from work. When she's doing something else.

DENISE: I see.

CASSIE: So you think something's wrong with that?

DENISE: Did I say that?

CASSIE: You're thinking it.

DENISE: So what if I am?

CASSIE: And what about your mom?

DENISE: What about her?

CASSIE: What does she think?

DENISE: I ... really don't know.

CASSIE: It's a little harder to disguise not eating, isn't it?

DENISE: Harder?

CASSIE: I mean I can fix extra stuff when my mom's not here.

DENISE: I guess she doesn't notice.

CASSIE: Doesn't notice.

DENISE: I nibble a little.

CASSIE: Nibble?

DENISE: At dinnertime. She doesn't notice. And then —

CASSIE: What?

DENISE: Like I said, the rest of the time it's just water.

CASSIE: You're going to get sick.

DENISE: Look who's talking.

CASSIE: It's a little more dangerous to starve yourself than to overeat.

DENISE: You've never heard of clogged arteries or heart attacks?

CASSIE: My God, Denise, I'm sixteen *[or her real age, if different]* years old.

DENISE: I hear about kids who have heart attacks. Athletes. Kids our age.

CASSIE: Because they're fat.

DENISE: Okay, you have a point.

CASSIE: Promise me you won't ...

DENISE: Won't what!

CASSIE: Won't overdo it.

DENISE: I'm not overdoing it.

CASSIE: Water all day and a few bites for dinner.

DENISE: I'll do all right. And what about you?

CASSIE: What about me?

DENISE: Stuffing yourself like that. It can't be good for you.

CASSIE: Maybe not. But once I gain all the weight I want —

DENISE: Yeah, and once I'm as thin as I want to be.

CASSIE: I try to keep exercising too. Exercises to build up the body.

DENISE: Me too. I exercise. *(Laughs.)* But not to build up my body.

CASSIE: Some day I'll have the kind of figure I want.

DENISE: Me too.

CASSIE: Wouldn't it be nice if we could just trade places? Well, talk to you tomorrow

(The lights fade to black and immediately come up again.)

SCENE 2

It is four months later.

NOTE: Throughout this scene, Denise picks up the cotton on the
floor and stuffs it back into the bag around her neck, and Cassie
slowly takes the cotton from her bag and places it on the floor.

(The phone rings in Denise's room. She picks up the receiver.)

DENISE: Hello.

CASSIE: Hi, Denise.

DENISE: Cassie! What's up?

CASSIE: It worked, didn't it?

DENISE: What worked?

CASSIE: The diets.

DENISE: Yeah. Worked great. I look just like I wanted.

CASSIE: Me too. Just what I wanted.

DENISE: Put on some weight, huh?

CASSIE: I did.

DENISE: Me too. I mean I lost some weight.

CASSIE: We did it. We worked at it and did it.

DENISE: Yeah. Got a whole new wardrobe.

CASSIE: Me too. Lot of new clothes. That was the good part.

DENISE: Good part?

CASSIE: Yeah. All those new clothes.

DENISE: Me too. Lot of new clothes.

CASSIE: Denise?

DENISE: Yeah?

CASSIE: You know what?

DENISE: What?

CASSIE: I envy you.

DENISE: Envy me?

CASSIE: Yeah ... I do.

DENISE: Because I lost weight.

CASSIE: No ... well, not exactly.

DENISE: I know what you mean. I guess ... well, I envy you, too.

CASSIE: I kept my old clothes.

DENISE: Kept your old clothes?

CASSIE: I don't know why. Not that I'll probably ever wear them again.

DENISE: I know. Me too. I'd never wear them again.

CASSIE: So did you get rid of your old —

DENISE: I kept my clothes too.

CASSIE: You did?

DENISE: Yeah.

CASSIE: Well, me, too.

DENISE: I know.

CASSIE: Why'd you keep your old clothes?

DENISE: Well, you know.

CASSIE: No.

DENISE: I just wanted — I don't — *(Accusingly)* You kept yours!

CASSIE: That's what I said.

DENISE: Yeah. So ...

CASSIE: Yes?

DENISE: Why'd you keep yours?

CASSIE: Gee, I ... Kind of silly, I suppose.

DENISE: No!

CASSIE: No?

DENISE: No, it's not silly.

CASSIE: You're right.

DENISE: Oh, gosh. I do envy you.

CASSIE: Me? You envy me?

DENISE: We shouldn't have done it, should we?

CASSIE: No. Well, they say the grass is always greener.

DENISE: I feel like a bag of bones.

CASSIE: I feel like a two-ton truck.

DENISE: I'm going to go on a diet.

CASSIE: Me too. I'm going to go on a diet too.

DENISE: See you tomorrow.

CASSIE: Sleep tight.

> *(DENISE and CASSIE hang up the phones. DENISE frantically stuffs her bag while CASSIE frantically throws cotton out of hers. The lights fade to black.)*

CURTAIN

Finally, here are two scenes from a play called *The Prank*.

Cast of Characters:
BILL POLSKY, 17
MARSHA PEREZ, attorney, 29-34
LIEUTENANT PAULA HABERMAN, 39

SETTING: The action occurs at various locations in Somerset
    County, Pennsylvania

SCENE 2

AT RISE: We are in the office of attorney MARSHA PEREZ, who is
    seated behind a large oak desk. BILL POLSKY sits in a padded
    chair in front of the desk.

PEREZ: I'm going to be your attorney, Bill. Do you understand?
BILL: Yeah.
PEREZ: So I have to ask a few questions.
BILL: Okay.
PEREZ: For the record, what's your name?
BILL: Bill Polsky. William Richard Polsky
PEREZ: Where do you live, Bill?
BILL: In Somerset. Somerset, P.A. At 226 South Broadway.
PEREZ: How old are you?
BILL: Seventeen. I'd have been a senior in high school, except ...
PEREZ: Yes?
BILL: I quit. I hate that school.
PEREZ: Why do you hate it?
BILL: Because of what happened.
PEREZ: Can you tell me?
BILL: It wasn't my fault. I didn't know Jimmy and Rich were
    planning something like that. And then ... *(His voice breaks.)*
PEREZ: We can stop for awhile, if you like.
BILL: No!
PEREZ: Till you ... feel better.

BILL: I'm all right! *(Beat)* Sorry. But they were my two best friends. My only friends. So afterwards ... After it was over and I was walking down the hall between classes, I kept expecting to hear their voices. I'd go to the cafeteria and start to save seats.

PEREZ: It wasn't till later that they discovered the body?

BILL: The body?

PEREZ: The man? The one who ... shot them.

BILL: The one I beat to death? Go ahead and say it.

PEREZ: I know this must be difficult.

BILL: It was ten days later. He lived alone. Then people started to wonder, I guess. They got concerned.

PEREZ: And so the police went to look.

BILL: Yeah.

PEREZ: But they'd found the two boys!

BILL: *(Sarcastically)* Yeah, the two boys.

PEREZ: How could they —

BILL: You didn't know?

PEREZ: I'm sorry.

BILL: I carried them to the car. Jimmy's car. I wasn't thinking straight. I just felt I had to get them out of there. Away from — It doesn't make sense. I know that. I took them to school and — *(He breaks down.)*

PEREZ: You took them to school?

BILL: *(Fighting for control)* And took them out and laid them on the ground. They were cold. I knew they were dead.

PEREZ: But you took them to school. Why would you do that?

BILL: I don't know.

SCENE 3

AT RISE: We are at the farm formerly owned by Mr. Summers.
Police LIEUTENANT PAULA HABERMAN and BILL POLSKY
are standing in an open field beside the farmhouse.

PAULA: Can you tell me what happened?

BILL: I really can't tell you ...

PAULA: Can't tell me?

BILL: I didn't want to go with them. But I had to. I didn't want them
to think ...

PAULA: I'm not condemning you. I'm trying to discover what
happened.

BILL: It was a joke. A dumb ... prank. For Halloween. We didn't
know anything was going to happen. You know Mr. Summers
... He always ...

PAULA: Yes. Always what?

BILL: The guy had been hurt before. Did anyone tell you that?

PAULA: You're the first one I've talked with.

BILL: Not him exactly. But his wife. Somebody hurt his wife real
bad. A long time ago. I didn't know that then.

PAULA: What did he do? Can you tell me exactly?

BILL: We were moving his outhouse. Just as a joke, like I said. But
I don't know what he thought was going on. He came out of
the house with that shotgun, screaming at us. I took off
running, but Jimmy and Rich turned toward him, maybe like
they were going to apologize. God! I don't know.

PAULA: Take your time.

BILL: He shot them. Like they were nothin'. He killed them.

PAULA: Bill. Did you see the actual shooting?

BILL: I heard it. I heard shots. And I turned, and he was standing
there. Staring.

PAULA: Staring?

BILL: Yeah.

PAULA: What do you mean?

BILL: At Jimmy and Rich. Lying there. I screamed and ran toward

174

them. It was like he hadn't realized what he'd done. "Oh, God, he yelled. "Oh, God!" He threw the shotgun as hard as he could. Raised it above his head and threw it into the field.

PAULA: Weren't you afraid, Bill?

BILL: I couldn't believe it. I was numb. It was my friends, lieutenant.

PAULA: I'm sorry. *(Beat)* But I have to continue.

BILL: I know you do.

PAULA: So what did you do?

BILL: I ran toward him and threw myself on top of him, and we fell.

PAULA: You threw him to the ground?

BILL: And I kept on hitting him. I couldn't stop. It was like someone else was inside me. Someone else, controlling what I did.

PAULA: You kept on beating him.

BILL: All I could think of was my friends. My friends lying there ... probably dead.

PAULA: But you didn't check?

BILL: No! Do you ... Do you think if I hadn't done what I did ... to Mr. Summers. Do you think ... If I'd gone to them first they might be alive.

PAULA: I didn't mean to imply that. With the injuries they sustained —

BILL: Sustained! Sustained?

PAULA: Maybe I've been a detective too long.

BILL: What?

PAULA: It was an awful thing for you. To have to go through. *(Beat)* You can't let yourself get involved. But you do get involved.

BILL: But if I could have helped them! *(Beat)* I'd do anything to make it different. You know I would!

After you play the scene or scenes in your own words, go back and see if you followed the ideas. Let the rest of the class point out anything you missed.

Improv based on an existing play can help in other ways as well. For instance, directors often have actors improvise a new scene that is not included in the play but which uses the same characters. The idea is to take the characters out of the context of the play to see how well you know them. When you do this sort of improvisation, you can add anything that is consistent with what you already know but which is not mentioned in the play. If you know the character well enough to understand how the person would act in a variety of situations outside of the play itself, this can make you secure in playing the character in a written drama.

Another sort of improv that helps an actor understand existing characters is to stage a character interview. Now, however, instead of creating an original character, fellow actors and the director can ask you any questions dealing with the character you are playing. This, similar to the last exercise, can help you flesh out the character and make him or her come alive.

Chapter Thirteen

Using Improv to Write Original Plays

Many successful plays have begun as improvisations. Sometimes the actors begin with an idea or a character or a simple plot. Even scenes that have their beginning in an improv performance provide a spark that indicates they may be the basis for a play.

Beginning with a Premise

Just as there are any number of ways you can begin an improv scene, there are many ways you can begin to improvise a play. The idea may come from an audience member who gives you a premise, "Summer Vacation." Of course, you can't deal with all of this in one play. It's too big a topic. So you have to narrow it. You have to improvise a scene or a monolog which sounds like it could be the basis of a one-act or full-length play. You add characters and scenes and a theme. Maybe it's a sinister sort of thing where someone is deliberately trying to drown people. Maybe it's about a summer romance that had to end or about a summer job that turned out differently than expected. Whatever it is, you improvise one scene and another and another.

Beginning with a Character Interview

There are many other ways to begin, as well. A good one is the character interview. The scenes from the play "The Prank" had their basis in two interviews, one with the character who emerged as Bill Polsky, the other as Paula Haberman. The original character interviews follow. You can see that in the first scene the character interview was changed only a little bit. The "Questioners" became the character of Marsha. Here is the interview:

Q: Hi.
A: Yeah, what do you want?
Q: To ask you a few questions.
A: Go on.
Q: What's your name?
A: Bill Polsky.
Q: Where do you live?
A: Somerset, P.A.
Q: Do you like it there?
A: It's way out in the sticks.
Q: Why do you stay?
A: Mom and Dad won't let me leave till I'm eighteen.
Q: How old are you?
A: Seventeen, okay? I'd have been a senior in high school, except ...
Q: Yes?
A: I quit. I hate that school.
Q: Why do you hate it?
A: Because of what happened.
Q: What do you mean?
A: It wasn't my fault. I didn't even know Jimmy and Rich planned to do anything. And then...
Q: Are you crying?
A: No! Yeah, I am. So what? You'd cry too. They were my two best friends. My only friends. So, you know, afterwards... After it was all over and I was walking down the hall between classes, I kept expecting to hear their voices. Or I'd go to the cafeteria and start to save seats. Then I'd remember. So I'm getting out of here, as soon as I can.

You can tell that it was not established in the interview that Bill's friends were killed nor that he attacked the farmer. However, we have seeds for those two things. The additional "facts" were logical outcomes of the interview; they were consistent with what was established.

It is natural then that someone investigate what happened.

Thus emerged the character of Paula, also developed through a character interview. Then the two characters were put together in a scene, which was changed and developed further. The scene was expanded. The original ended with Paula's lines, "Did you actually see the shooting?" The first part was polished and sharpened but essentially remained the same as in the interview.

So it often works to begin with one character and add other characters to support or expand upon various things the first character said. In "The Prank" the next character to be developed was the detective. After that came Bill's parents, Paula's ex-husband, and a number of other characters with smaller roles.

Beginning with a Setting

Another way to begin is with a setting. One person can present a monolog about it or you can do word association where one person says, "city," for instance. Others say, "ritzy area," "near the beach," "a mansion with servants," and so on. Then you improvise a scene or a monolog that occurs there.

> I never saw a place like that before. Big with giant pines in the yard and a big sliding gate. By the gate was a guard and a mean-looking police dog. I wondered why they were there. Where the people who lived here so afraid of being robbed? Or maybe they were afraid of being found out. But for what? I thought maybe they were international thieves. Members of the jet set who traveled all over the world committing burglaries.

This sort of monolog is almost like using stream of consciousness, that is, saying whatever comes into your head. In all probability this sort of thing would never be performed in front of an audience.

Yet in the monolog, you can see several possibilities. Maybe this is a comedy about these wealthy thieves whom nobody could possibly suspect of being burglars. Their families have been wealthy for years, but maybe they squandered all the money and have come up with what they think is a fool-proof way to maintain their lifestyle.

Then you begin to develop the characters, either through the character interviews or by arbitrarily giving them names and then putting them in a scene together where they are planning to rob a famous museum in London. From here you develop the plot further.

Beginning with a Trait

You also can begin improvising a play by listing a physical or emotional trait as a premise or an idea to build upon. For instance, you think of the word "greedy." How are you going to show this? Give the greedy person a name and put him or her in a scene with another character. Taking into consideration that you want to reveal the trait of greediness, just let the characters begin to talk.

PETER: Aunt Helen didn't leave me anything but this in her will?

JOAN: I thought you always liked her collection of silver figurines.

PETER: I didn't say I didn't. It's just that she always said I was her favorite nephew.

JOAN: Gosh, Peter, the woman is dead. Our aunt is dead, and all you can think about is what she left you!

PETER: I expected more, that's all. I don't like this. I'm going to fight the will, you know?

JOAN: Fight the will?

PETER: Go to court. Why should her kids get everything?

JOAN: Because they're her kids. Besides, they didn't get everything. You got the silver, and I got her Mercedes.

PETER: Why didn't I get the Mercedes?

JOAN: I can't believe this is my own brother talking!

Where would the action take place? Maybe at Aunt Helen's house...the mansion from which the jewel thieves operate. Maybe you can even tie that situation and this one together. Peter talks his cousins into operating the burglary ring. He tries to talk Joan into it too, but she refuses. Now the plot becomes a little more complicated. What does Joan do when she realizes what Peter and their cousins are up to?

Beginning with a Combination of Traits

You can have each person in class list a different trait: thin, compassionate, handsome, lazy, emotional, strong-willed, and so on. Then develop a character by choosing two or three of these traits and tying them together, maybe in a monolog:

Uncle Charlie had to be the *laziest* man I ever met. I remember when I was a kid and he was in college he'd come home every weekend and sack out till one or two on Saturday afternoon. Nothing could budge him from his bed, neither threats nor promises. Like the one time just to see if he'd do it, my dad, Uncle Charlie's brother, said he'd give him twenty dollars if he got up before nine. Now nine isn't all that bad, is it? I mean most people in school or with jobs are up long before that, at least on weekdays. But Uncle Charlie wouldn't do it. The thing was, he woke up early that Saturday and just lay there. He was so *strong-willed*.

But I liked Uncle Charlie. Even back then, especially back then, he really cared about people. The only good word to use to describe him is *compassionate*. Once one of my friends got in trouble at home. And his parents kicked him out. They said they didn't want him anymore. And that's pretty traumatic. Parents telling you to get out and not come back. Especially when you're fifteen or

181

> sixteen. My folks sympathized, but we couldn't take him in because we didn't have the room. Uncle Charlie said he would though. He'd be willing to move to a bigger place, and Donnie could stay with him. By then Uncle Charlie was in graduate school. He said that he'd get a part-time job at the college library or something to make up the difference in rent and expenses
>
> Now this was a sacrifice, getting a job, I mean, since, like I told you, Uncle Charlie didn't often exert himself when he didn't have to.
>
> So he took Donnie in until he finished high school, no strings attached.

You see that an interesting character begins to emerge. And this in turn suggests other characters — the person telling the story, Charlie's parents and his brother, and the boy Donnie. Maybe even Donnie's parents. And you have a couple of settings: Charlie's home and his apartment, and maybe the college.

The idea is to let things flow as you would in any improv. Then take what you have and add to it. If you don't like the character, the situation, or the location, begin again. Just as the character interview, this sort of thing takes little time to do, and it's not at all difficult.

When you develop a character like this, you may find that he is not the central character at all. Rather another character is much more interesting. Maybe it's Donnie; maybe you decide that you want to write a play about him. About his relationship with his parents and why they kicked him out.

Beginning with Random Words

You can begin with a list of random words, nouns or adjectives, as you did earlier in the book to come up with an idea for an improv. In a group, each person should say the first word that comes to mind, such as "dog," "lamp," and "season." Then in a scene or a monolog, tie the words together.

MOM: You'll have to get that *dog* out of here. That's all there is to it. If you can't control him, you can't have him in the house.

KIM: I can't just kick him out.

MOM: He jumps all over the furniture. He knocked over my *lamp*. That's an expensive lamp, Kim.

KIM: He didn't break it

MOM: Lucky he didn't. That's all I can say.

KIM: I'm sorry.

MOM: One more stunt like that, and that dog's not coming into my house.

KIM: Your house! I live here too.

MOM: Maybe you do, but not the dog.

KIM: But it's cold, and I don't know where I'll keep him.

MOM: Neither the *season* of the year nor where you'd keep him is my problem. And now the subject is closed.

A lot of tension developed in the scene, tension that suggests future action, a further building toward a climax. Maybe Kim, who comes across as young, takes the dog and runs away. It's wintertime, and the weather obviously is cold. So what happens then? That's what you have to decide by doing more scenes or monologs related to what you already have.

Beginning with an Object

The scene suggested by the basketball can be the basis of a play. Or you can take any other object and use it as the basis of an improv. Maybe it's a wallet.

RUTH: I wish I'd never found that wallet.

TERRY: Why, for heaven's sake?

RUTH: It's been nothing but trouble.

TERRY: In what way?

RUTH: First of all, there were all these people trying to claim it.

TERRY: After you put the ad in the paper.

RUTH: I didn't realize how many dishonest people there are in this world.

TERRY: People who tried to tell you the wallet was theirs.

RUTH: You wouldn't believe the sob stories.

TERRY: But you found the person who lost it?

RUTH: Yes, unfortunately.

TERRY: Unfortunately! But you said it contained a lot of money.

RUTH: That's right.

TERRY: Wasn't that man ...

RUTH: His name is Ron.

TERRY: Wasn't Ron glad to get it back?

RUTH: Oh, he was glad all right. Too glad, as a matter of fact. Now he won't leave me alone.

TERRY: In what way?

RUTH: You know the Chinese are supposed to have this belief that if you save a person's life, you're responsible for that person from then on.

TERRY: What's that got to do with anything?

RUTH: I think that's how Ron feels about the wallet!

TERRY: That you're responsible for his wallet.

RUTH: That I'm responsible for him. He lost his job.

TERRY: As well as his wallet?

RUTH: Ummm. And he keeps calling and dropping by all the time.

TERRY: Sounds interesting. What's he like?

RUTH: Oh, he's all right, I guess.

TERRY: All right.

RUTH: Okay, I think he's an attractive man.

TERRY: So what's the problem?

RUTH: I'm not responsible for him, Terry, no matter what he thinks. Or you think.

TERRY: Hey, now wait a minute here. *(Beat)* Didn't Shakespeare write a line that fits the situation?

RUTH: What line?

TERRY: Methinks the lady doth protest too much.

A situation is beginning to emerge, one that, it develops, has comic overtones. So maybe the play could point that out. It could be a comedy involving Ruth and Ron. Since Terry doesn't really play any important role here, you may want to drop her. On the other hand, she could be Ruth's best friend and confidante. The action could take place, at least in part, in Ruth's home, which is suggested in the scene. And, of course, a character who is strongly suggested for the play is Ron.

Beginning with a Situation

Almost any sort of situation can be the basis for a play. Let's suppose it's a phone that doesn't ring.

TINA: I wish that phone would ring.

HANK: The waiting's tough, isn't it?

TINA: *(Sarcastically)* Good old Hank. Always there with a sympathetic word.

HANK: I do what I can. *(Pause)* He should have been there by now?

TINA: He should have been there hours ago.

HANK: Could he have been delayed? Could it just have slipped his mind that he promised to call?

TINA: It's not like him, Hank. In all the years we've been together, he never failed to call me.

Here you have the beginnings of a sort of mystery. Tina is worried about someone. Who is it? Someone obviously close to her. A husband probably. But if it's her husband, who is Hank? A good friend, a neighbor, her brother.

If you wanted to develop it into a play, you could go on with the same scene to see what happens, to see if the phone eventually rings, or you could arbitrarily decide that the person Tina misses is her husband. Then you need to figure out why he didn't call. Did he and Tina have an argument? Did he, as Hank suggested, simply forget? Was he delayed?

When you ask questions like this, it helps clarify the situation. It's almost like the character interview, except there are no characters speaking. You're posing these questions to each other in a class where you're working to develop a play.

Beginning with Given Circumstances

At random you can come up with given circumstances, perhaps going around the room with each person adding a single "fact."

Location: "Los Angeles." "A slum area." "Used to be a nice neighborhood." "Outside on the street."

Characters: Juan, an eighteen-year-old high school dropout; Rachel, his girlfriend; Danny, his cousin; Maria, his mother; Sam Wilson, Juan's best friend; Jose, Juan's father; Lester Wilson, Sam's father.

Situation: Trouble between two street gangs.

Action: Juan rushes up to help Sam, who is kneeling on the sidewalk. Rachel is trying to pull Juan away.

You don't need to use all the characters suggested, or you may want to add others. But you do have to come up with a reason for the situation and the action. You more clearly have to define what is happening. You can use all the other techniques you know to help with this: doing monologs or scenes, working with an object, and so on.

Beginning with Two Unrelated Actions

At random think of two unrelated actions and tie them together. This is similar to using a combination of traits in that you try to go from one to the other in a logical way.

A young man is playing baseball.
A young woman is eating lunch in a cafeteria.

How might you tie these together? How are they logically related? The young man hits a ball that smashes through the window of the cafeteria, landing in the woman's soup. She is very angry because she has used her last dollar to buy a meal which now is ruined. She comes outside and screams at the young man. He thinks she's hurt and goes to investigate. From there you can go any number of ways. Or you can come up with many other different scenarios to fit the two actions.

Developing the Play

The point is, you can use lots of techniques for developing a play. It doesn't matter which one or which combination. You just need to keep coming up with different scenes and characters and directions to see what works best. Maybe by the time you finish the play will be nothing like what it was in the beginning, or maybe it will include nearly everything you've come up with.

During the early stages, each time you and the others get together in your group to work on the play, try something different, a new scene or a new character, perhaps.

Finally, you should come to an agreement on what you like and on the direction of the play. Then it's a matter of taking the scenes you like and reworking them, playing them again and again till they are pretty well set. Then you can write them down. Soon you'll have a play.

Selected Bibliography

Atkins, Gary. *Improv!: A Handbook for the Actor*. Portsmouth, NH: Heinemann, 1995.

Caruso, Sandra and Paul Clemens. *The Actor's Book of Improvisation*. New York: Penguin Books, 1992.

Frost, Anthony and Ralph Yarrow. *Improvisation in Drama*. Basingstoke: Macmillan Education, 1990.

Goldberg, Andy. *Improv Comedy*. New York: Samuel French, 1991.

Halpern, Charna, Del Close and Kim "Howard" Johnson. *Truth in Comedy: The Manual of Improvisation*. Colorado Springs: Meriwether Publishing Ltd., 1994.

Izzo, Gary. *The Art of Play: The New Genre of Interactive Theatre*. Portsmouth, NH: Heinemann, 1997.

Jones, Brie. *Improve with Improv: A Guide to Improvisation and Character Development*. Colorado Springs: Meriwether Publishing Ltd., 1993.

Tufnell, Miranda and Chris Crickmay. *Body, Space, Image: Notes Towards Improvisation and Performance*. London: Virago, 1990.

About the Author

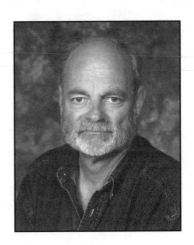

Marsh Cassady has written more than forty books including novels, short story and drama collections, haiku, biography and books on theatre and storytelling. His audio and stage plays have been widely performed (including off-Broadway) and he has written and recorded a three-set audio tape on storytelling.

A former actor/director and university professor with a Ph.D. degree in theatre, Cassady has worked with more than a hundred productions. Currently fiction/drama editor of *Crazyquilt Quarterly*, he was editor of both a regional and a national magazine. Since 1981 he has conducted an all-genre writing workshop in San Diego and has taught various creative writing classes at UCSD and elsewhere. While teaching at Montclair State in the 1970s, he started a program of workshops, classes and special projects in playwriting. His writing has won numerous regional and national awards.

Also by Marsh Cassady

Great Scenes from Women Playwrights
Characters in Action
The Theatre and You
Acting Games — Improvisations and Exercises
The Art of Storytelling
Great Scenes from Minority Playwrights
Funny Business

Order Form

Meriwether Publishing Ltd.
P.O. Box 7710
Colorado Springs, CO 80933
Telephone: (719) 594-4422
Website: www.meriwetherpublishing.com

Please send me the following books:

_____ **Spontaneous Performance #BK-B239**   **$15.95**
by Marsh Cassady
Acting through Improv

_____ **Acting Games — Improvisations and**   **$15.95**
Exercises #BK-B168
by Marsh Cassady
A textbook of theatre games and improvisations

_____ **Theatre Games for Young Performers #BK-B188**   **$16.95**
by Maria C. Novelly
Improvisations and exercises for developing acting skills

_____ **Theatre Games and Beyond #BK-B217**   **$16.95**
by Amiel Schotz
A creative approach for performers

_____ **Funny Business #BK-B212**   **$16.95**
by Marsh Cassady
An introduction to comedy

_____ **Improve with Improv! BK-B160**   **$14.95**
by Brie Jones
A guide to improvisation and character development

_____ **Truth in Comedy #BK-B164**   **$16.95**
by Charna Halpern, Del Close and Kim "Howard" Johnson
The guidebook of theatre fundamentals

These and other fine Meriwether Publishing books are available at
your local bookstore or direct from the publisher. Prices subject to
change without notice. Check our website or call for current prices.

Name: _____

Organization name: _____

Address: _____

City: _____ State: _____

Zip: _____ Phone: _____

❏ **Check enclosed**

❏ **Visa / MasterCard / Discover #** _____

Expiration
Signature: _____ *date:* _____
(required for Visa/MasterCard/Discover orders)

Colorado residents: Please add 3% sales tax.
Shipping: Include $2.75 for the first book and 50¢ for each additional book ordered.

❏ *Please send me a copy of your complete catalog of books and plays.*